nickelodeon

降击神通

AVATAR

THE LAST AIRBENDER

Created by
Bryan Konietzko
Michael Dante DiMartino

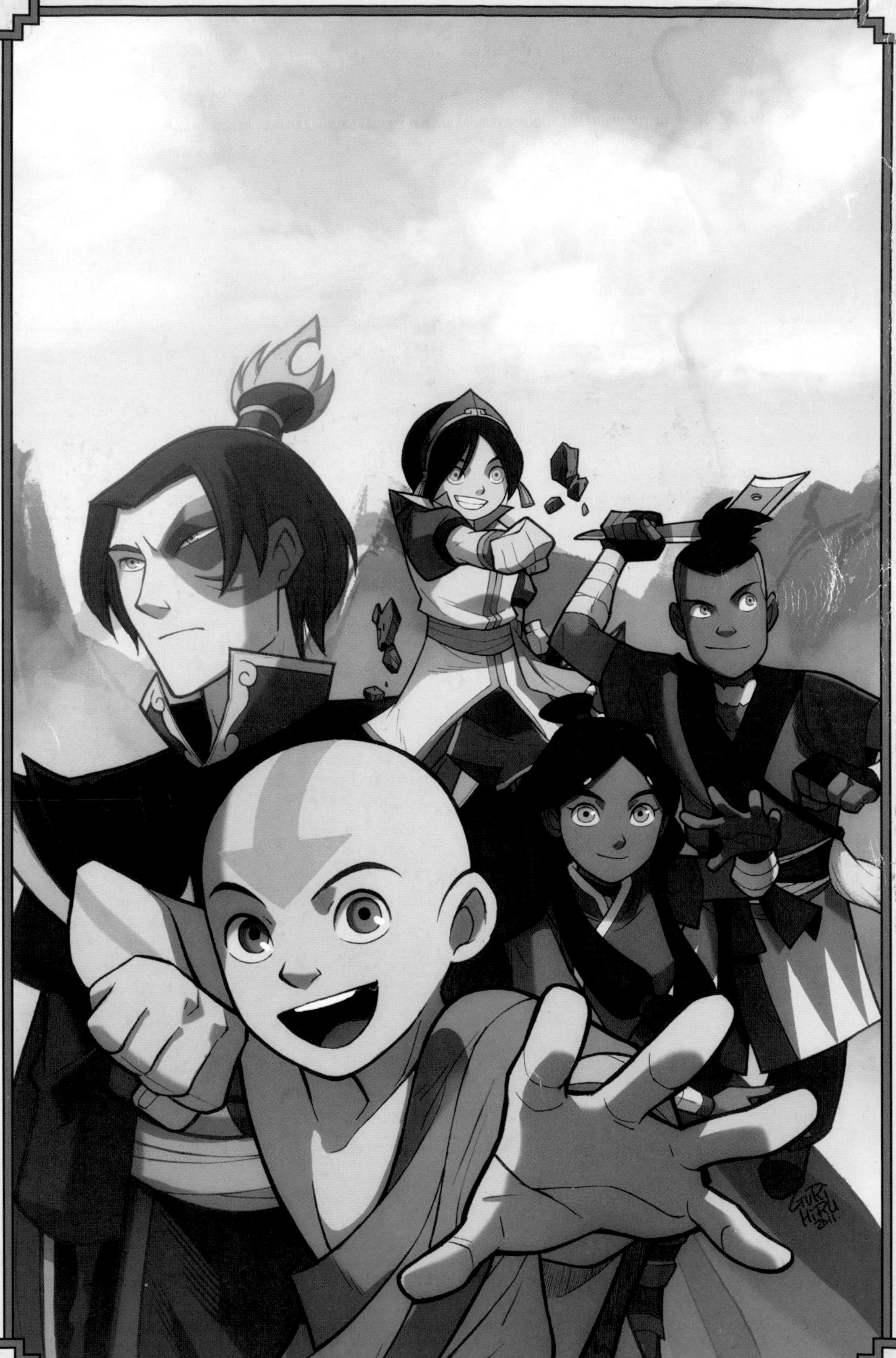
GURI HIRU 2011

nickelodeon

降击神通

AVATAR

THE LAST AIRBENDER

THE PROMISE · PART ONE

script
GENE LUEN YANG

art and cover
GURIHIRU

lettering
MICHAEL HEISLER

DARK HORSE BOOKS

publisher
MIKE RICHARDSON

designer
JUSTIN COUCH

assistant editor
BRENDAN WRIGHT

editor
DAVE MARSHALL

Special thanks to Linda Lee, Kat van Dam, James Salerno,
Brian Smith, and Joan Hilty at Nickelodeon, to Samantha Robertson,
and to Bryan Konietzko and Michael Dante DiMartino.

Nickelodeon Avatar: The Last Airbender™—The Promise Part 1

Published by
Dark Horse Books
A division of
Dark Horse Comics, Inc.
10956 SE Main Street
Milwaukie, OR 97222

DarkHorse.com
Nick.com

To find a comics shop in your area, call the Comic Shop
Locator Service toll-free at (888) 266-4226.

First edition: January 2012
ISBN 978-1-59582-811-8

7 9 10 8 6

Printed in China

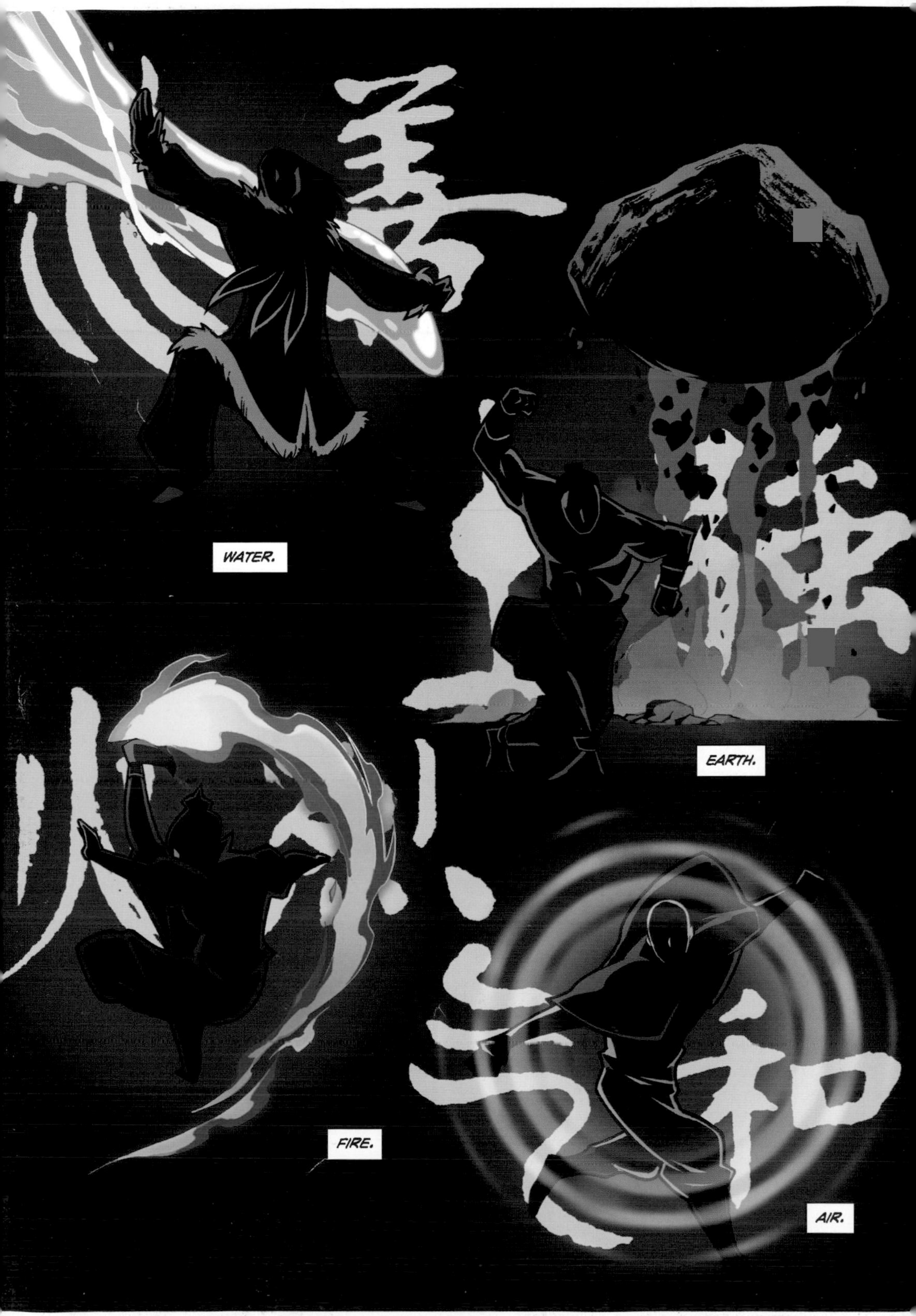
WATER.
EARTH.
FIRE.
AIR.

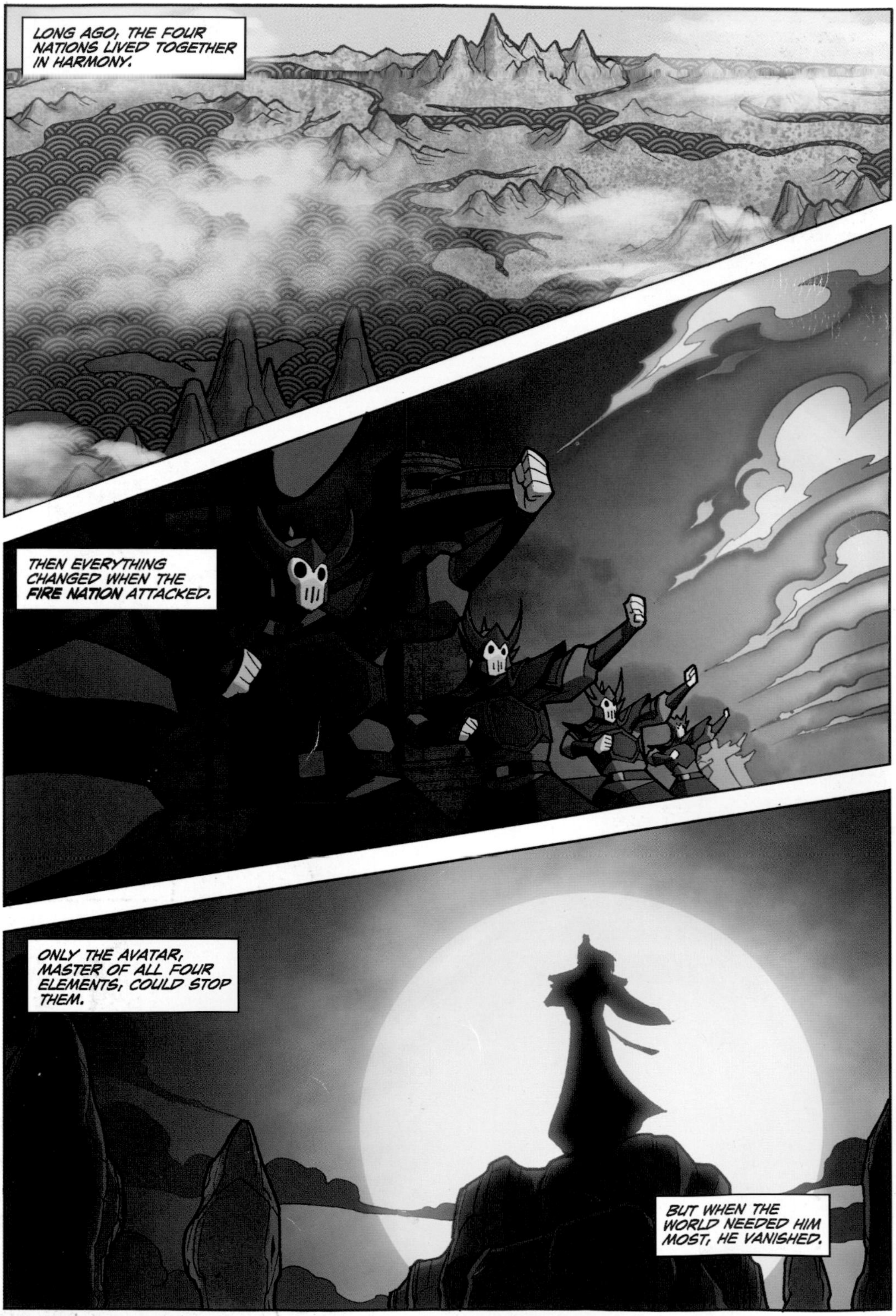
LONG AGO, THE FOUR NATIONS LIVED TOGETHER IN HARMONY.
THEN EVERYTHING CHANGED WHEN THE FIRE NATION ATTACKED.
ONLY THE AVATAR, MASTER OF ALL FOUR ELEMENTS, COULD STOP THEM.
BUT WHEN THE WORLD NEEDED HIM MOST, HE VANISHED.

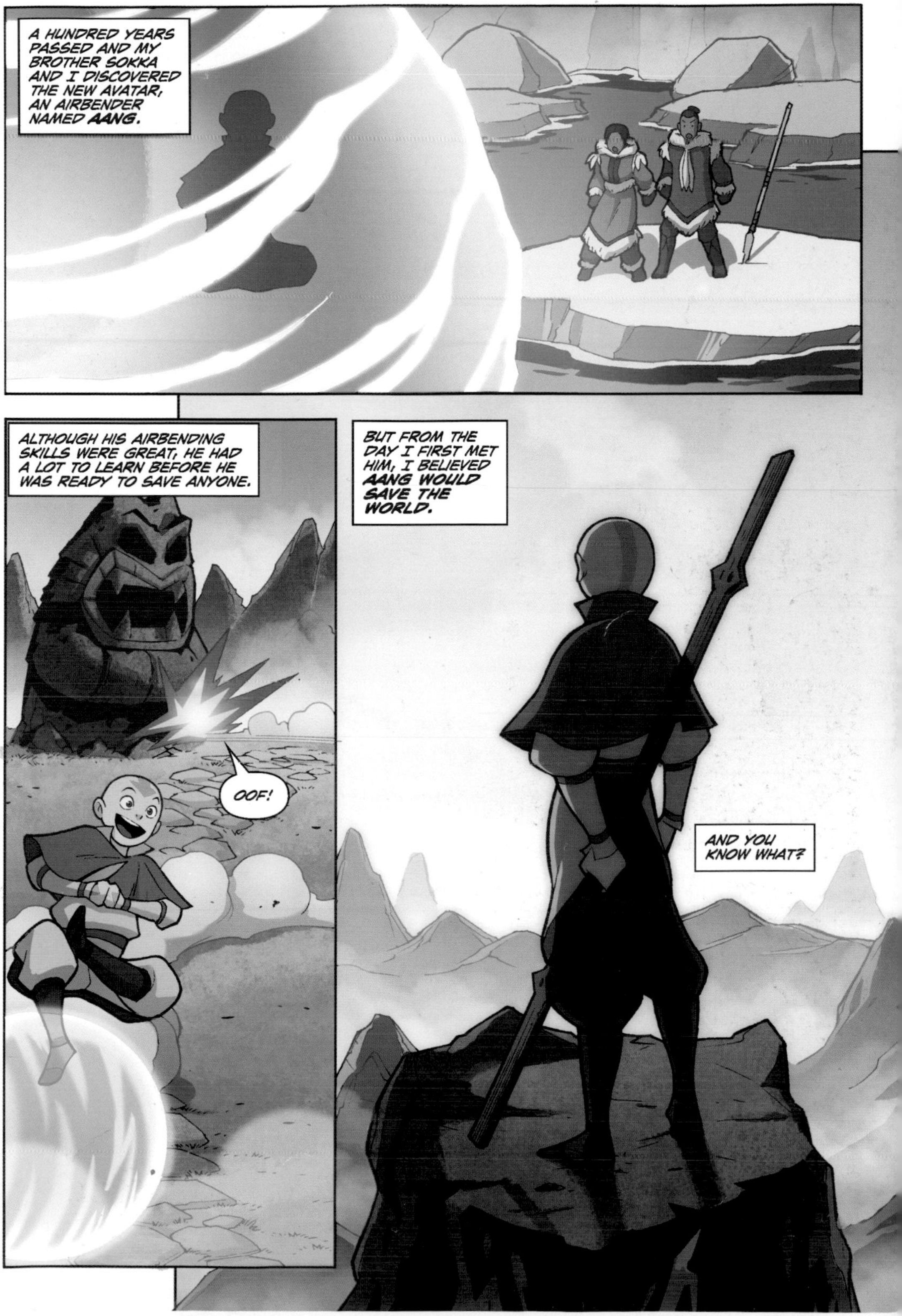
A HUNDRED YEARS PASSED AND MY BROTHER SOKKA AND I DISCOVERED THE NEW AVATAR, AN AIRBENDER NAMED **AANG**.
ALTHOUGH HIS AIRBENDING SKILLS WERE GREAT, HE HAD A LOT TO LEARN BEFORE HE WAS READY TO SAVE ANYONE.
OOF!
BUT FROM THE DAY I FIRST MET HIM, I BELIEVED **AANG WOULD SAVE THE WORLD**.
AND YOU KNOW WHAT?

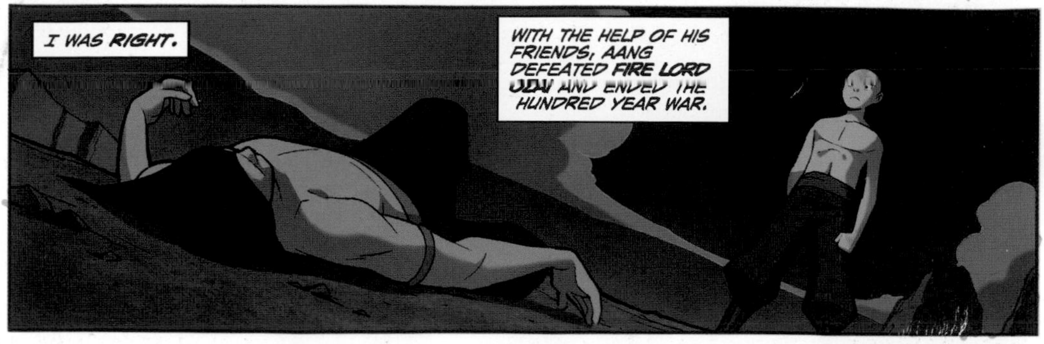
I WAS **RIGHT**.
WITH THE HELP OF HIS FRIENDS, AANG DEFEATED **FIRE LORD OZAI** AND ENDED THE HUNDRED YEAR WAR.

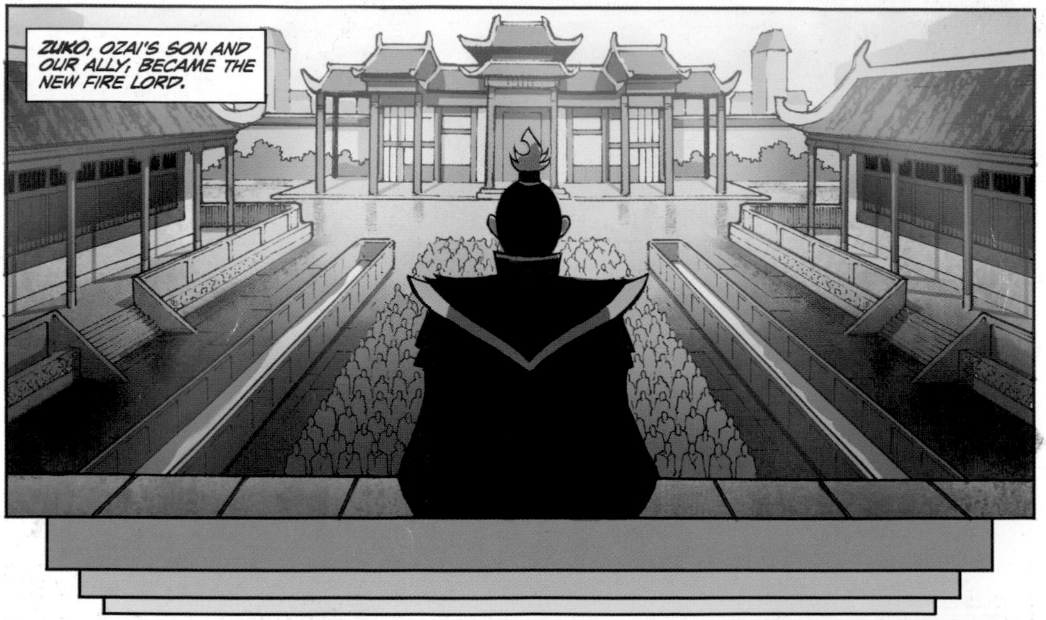
ZUKO, OZAI'S SON AND OUR ALLY, BECAME THE NEW FIRE LORD.

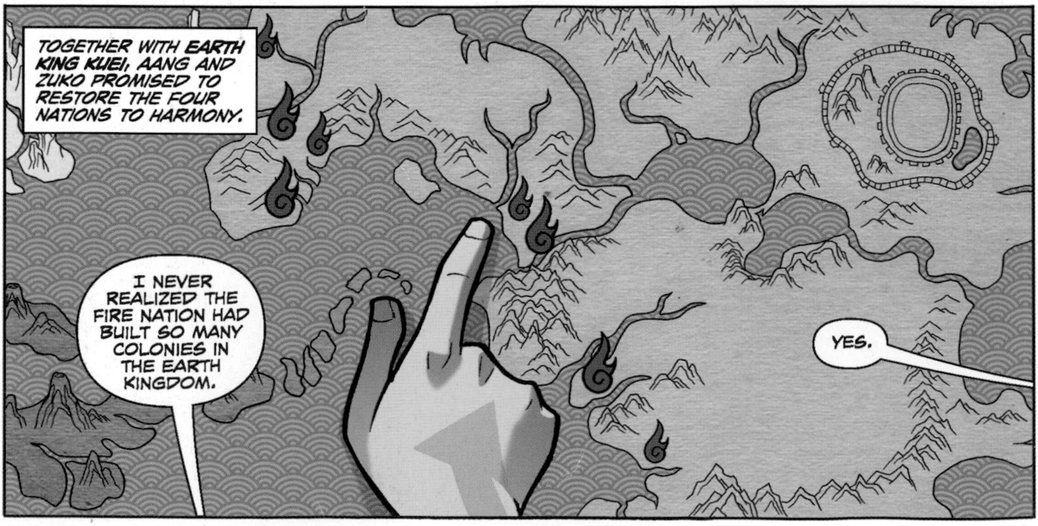
TOGETHER WITH **EARTH KING KUEI**, AANG AND ZUKO PROMISED TO RESTORE THE FOUR NATIONS TO HARMONY.
I NEVER REALIZED THE FIRE NATION HAD BUILT SO MANY COLONIES IN THE EARTH KINGDOM.
YES.

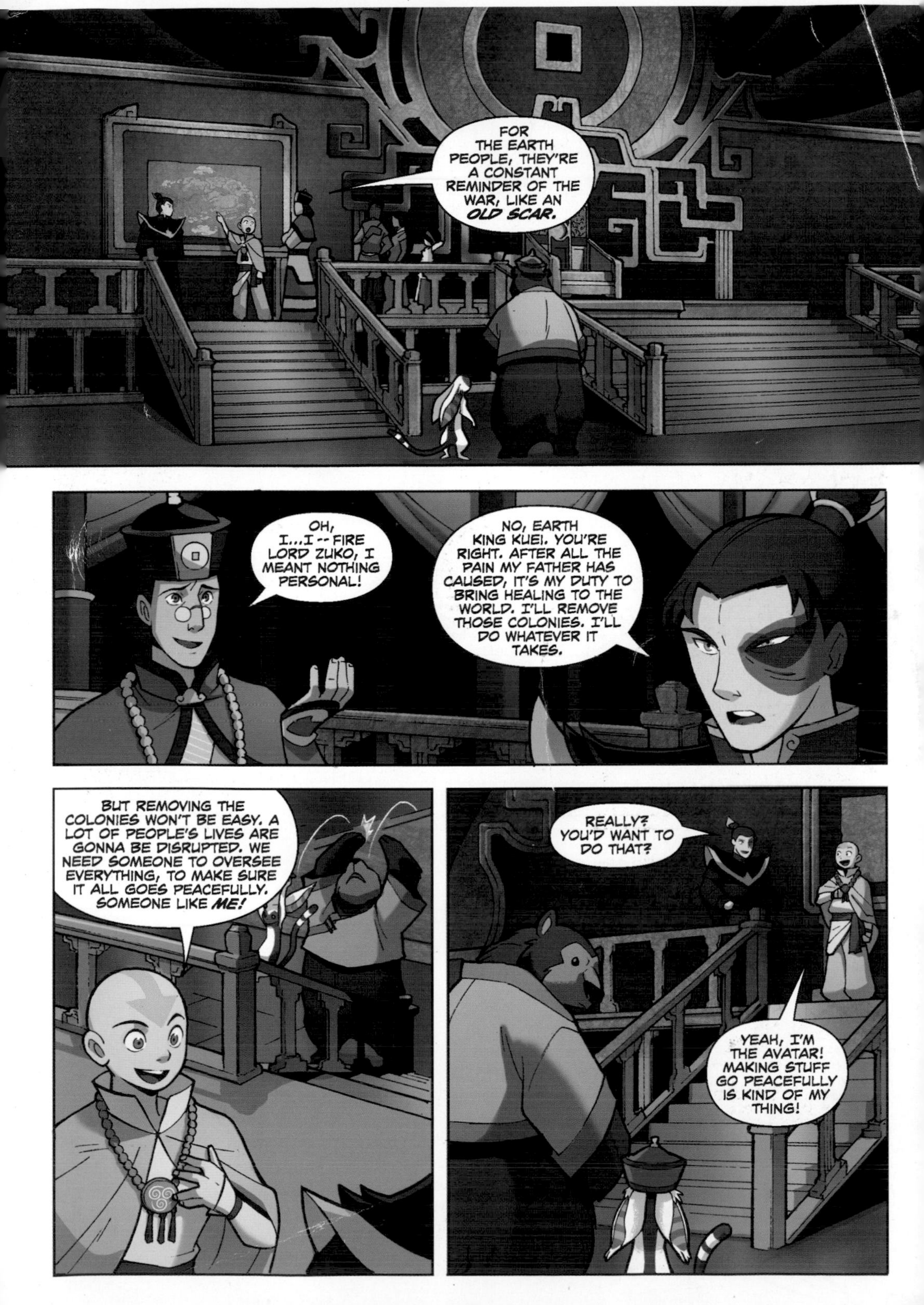

FOR THE EARTH PEOPLE, THEY'RE A CONSTANT REMINDER OF THE WAR, LIKE AN *OLD SCAR.*
OH, I...I -- FIRE LORD ZUKO, I MEANT NOTHING PERSONAL!
NO, EARTH KING KUEI. YOU'RE RIGHT. AFTER ALL THE PAIN MY FATHER HAS CAUSED, IT'S MY DUTY TO BRING HEALING TO THE WORLD. I'LL REMOVE THOSE COLONIES. I'LL DO WHATEVER IT TAKES.
BUT REMOVING THE COLONIES WON'T BE EASY. A LOT OF PEOPLE'S LIVES ARE GONNA BE DISRUPTED. WE NEED SOMEONE TO OVERSEE EVERYTHING, TO MAKE SURE IT ALL GOES PEACEFULLY. SOMEONE LIKE *ME!*
REALLY? YOU'D WANT TO DO THAT?
YEAH, I'M THE AVATAR! MAKING STUFF GO PEACEFULLY IS KIND OF MY THING!

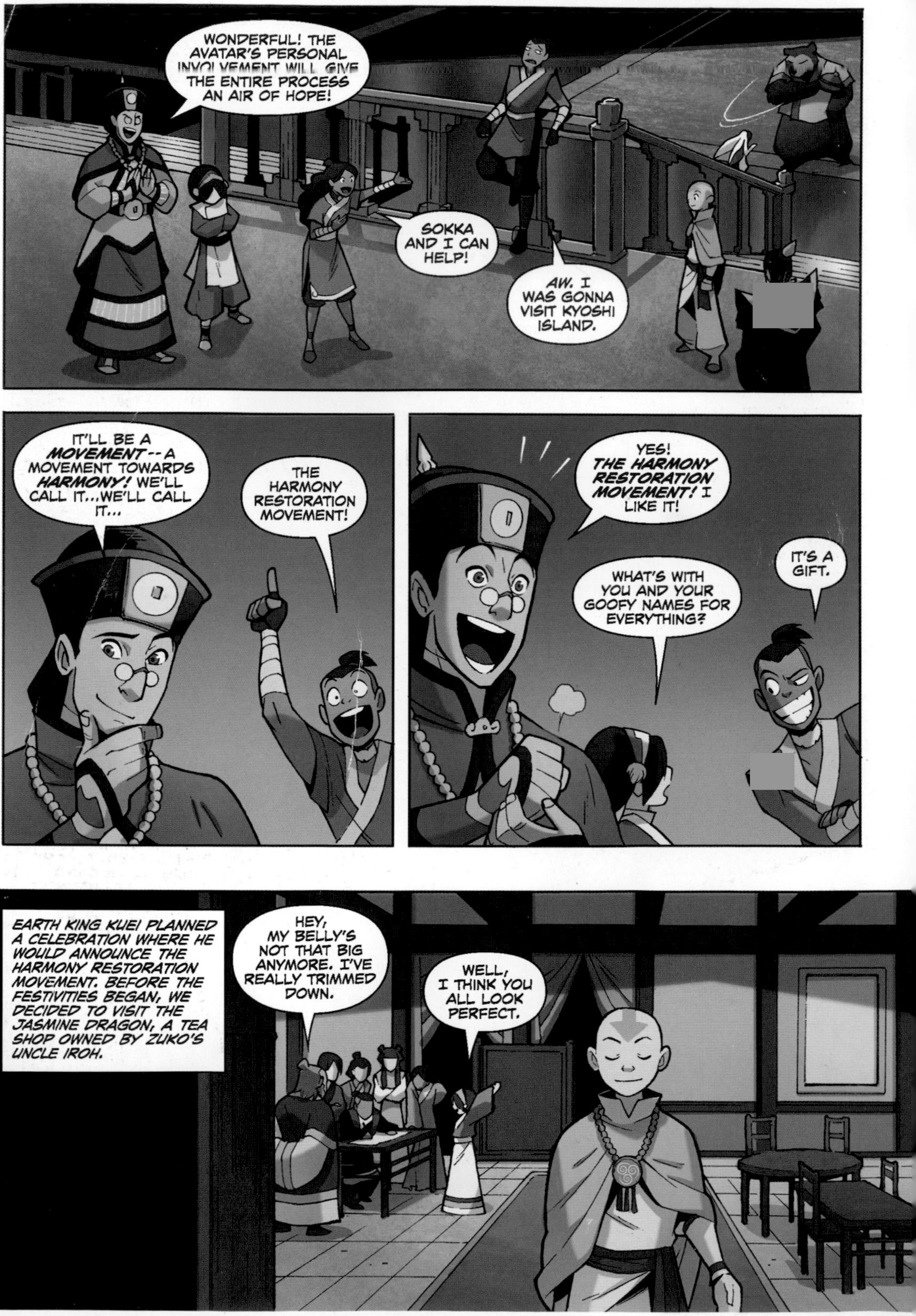
WONDERFUL! THE AVATAR'S PERSONAL INVOLVEMENT WILL GIVE THE ENTIRE PROCESS AN AIR OF HOPE!
SOKKA AND I CAN HELP!
AW. I WAS GONNA VISIT KYOSHI ISLAND.
IT'LL BE A MOVEMENT-- A MOVEMENT TOWARDS HARMONY! WE'LL CALL IT...WE'LL CALL IT...
THE HARMONY RESTORATION MOVEMENT!
YES! THE HARMONY RESTORATION MOVEMENT! I LIKE IT!
WHAT'S WITH YOU AND YOUR GOOFY NAMES FOR EVERYTHING?
IT'S A GIFT.
EARTH KING KUEI PLANNED A CELEBRATION WHERE HE WOULD ANNOUNCE THE HARMONY RESTORATION MOVEMENT. BEFORE THE FESTIVITIES BEGAN, WE DECIDED TO VISIT THE JASMINE DRAGON, A TEA SHOP OWNED BY ZUKO'S UNCLE IROH.
HEY, MY BELLY'S NOT THAT BIG ANYMORE. I'VE REALLY TRIMMED DOWN.
WELL, I THINK YOU ALL LOOK PERFECT.

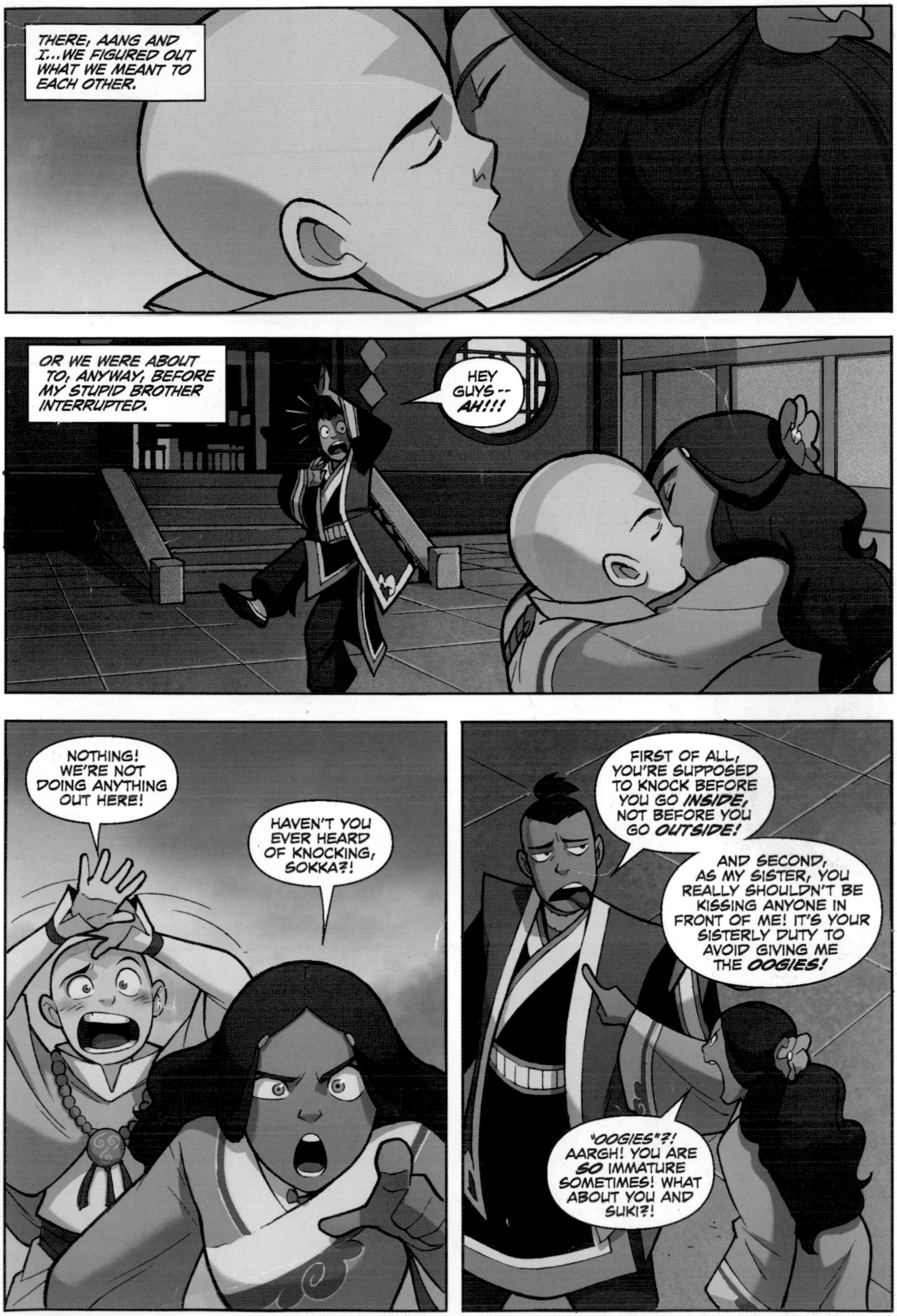
THERE, AANG AND I...WE FIGURED OUT WHAT WE MEANT TO EACH OTHER.
OR WE WERE ABOUT TO, ANYWAY, BEFORE MY STUPID BROTHER INTERRUPTED.
HEY GUYS -- AH!!!
NOTHING! WE'RE NOT DOING ANYTHING OUT HERE!
HAVEN'T YOU EVER HEARD OF KNOCKING, SOKKA?!
FIRST OF ALL, YOU'RE SUPPOSED TO KNOCK BEFORE YOU GO INSIDE, NOT BEFORE YOU GO OUTSIDE!
AND SECOND, AS MY SISTER, YOU REALLY SHOULDN'T BE KISSING ANYONE IN FRONT OF ME! IT'S YOUR SISTERLY DUTY TO AVOID GIVING ME THE OOGIES!
"OOGIES"?! AARGH! YOU ARE SO IMMATURE SOMETIMES! WHAT ABOUT YOU AND SUKI?!

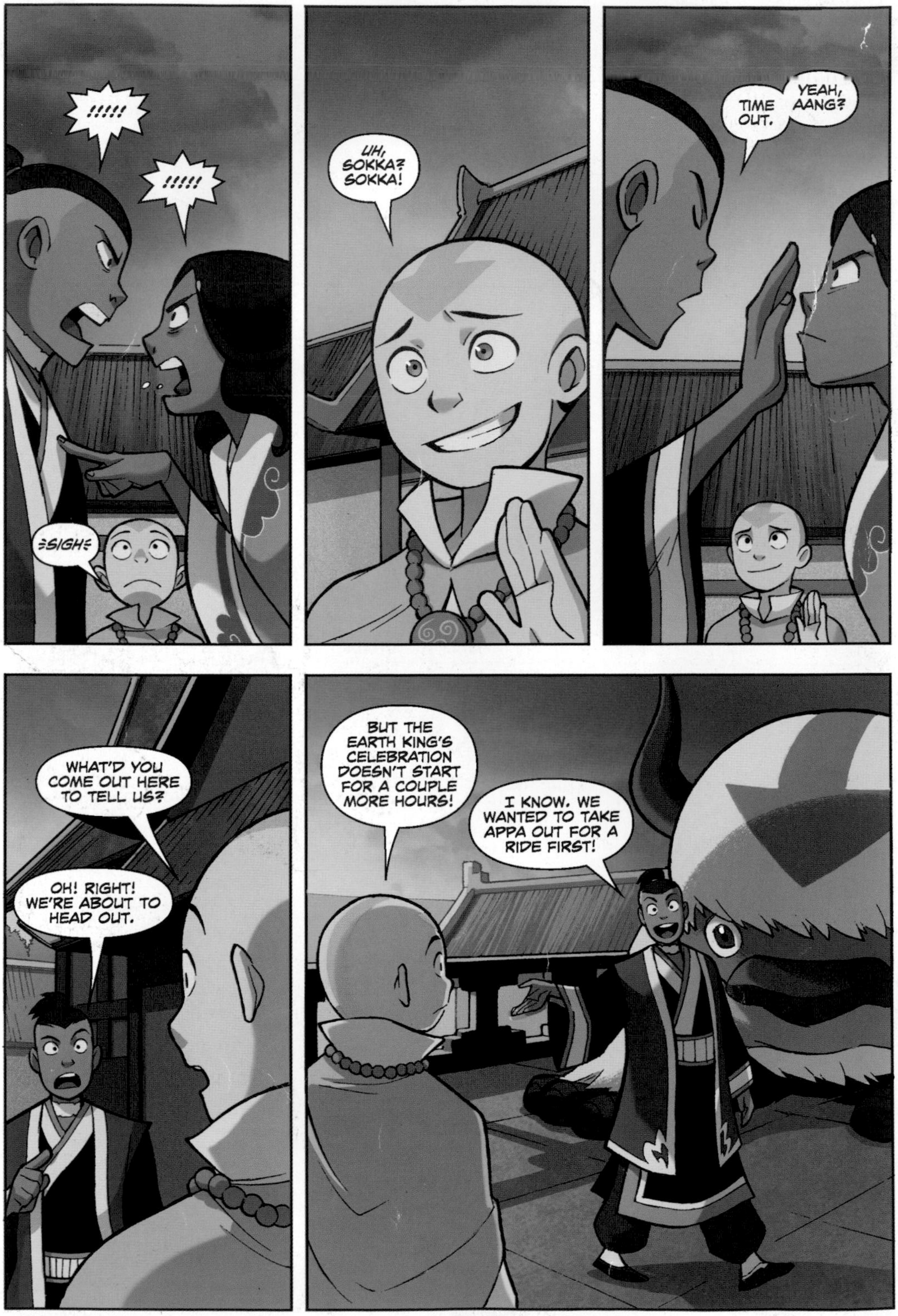
!!!!!
!!!!!
≈SIGH≈
UH, SOKKA? SOKKA!
TIME OUT.
YEAH, AANG?
WHAT'D YOU COME OUT HERE TO TELL US?
OH! RIGHT! WE'RE ABOUT TO HEAD OUT.
BUT THE EARTH KING'S CELEBRATION DOESN'T START FOR A COUPLE MORE HOURS!
I KNOW. WE WANTED TO TAKE APPA OUT FOR A RIDE FIRST!

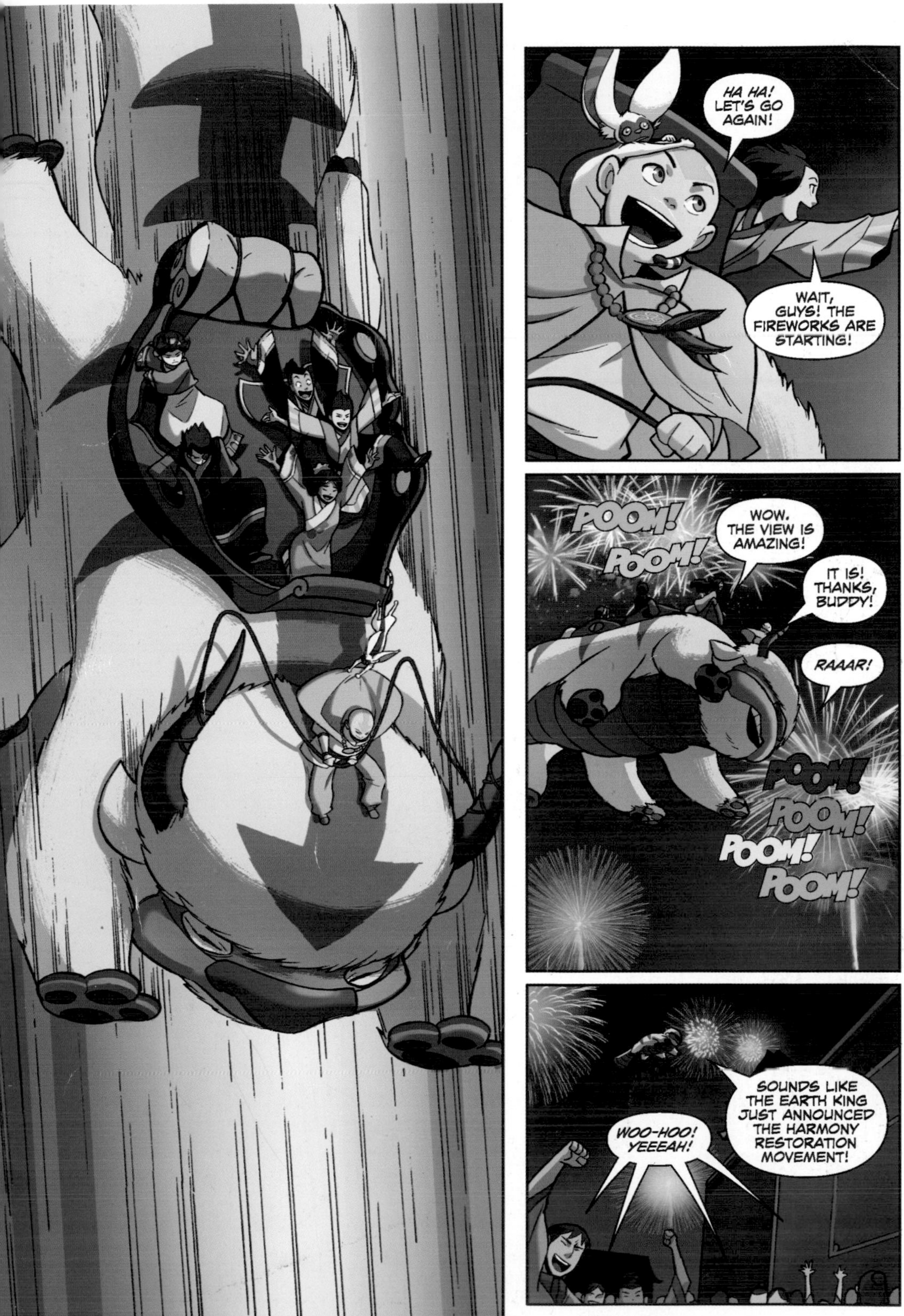
HA HA! LET'S GO AGAIN!
WAIT, GUYS! THE FIREWORKS ARE STARTING!
POOM!
POOM!
WOW. THE VIEW IS AMAZING!
IT IS! THANKS, BUDDY!
RAAAR!
POOM!
POOM!
POOM!
POOM!
SOUNDS LIKE THE EARTH KING JUST ANNOUNCED THE HARMONY RESTORATION MOVEMENT!
WOO-HOO! YEEEAH!

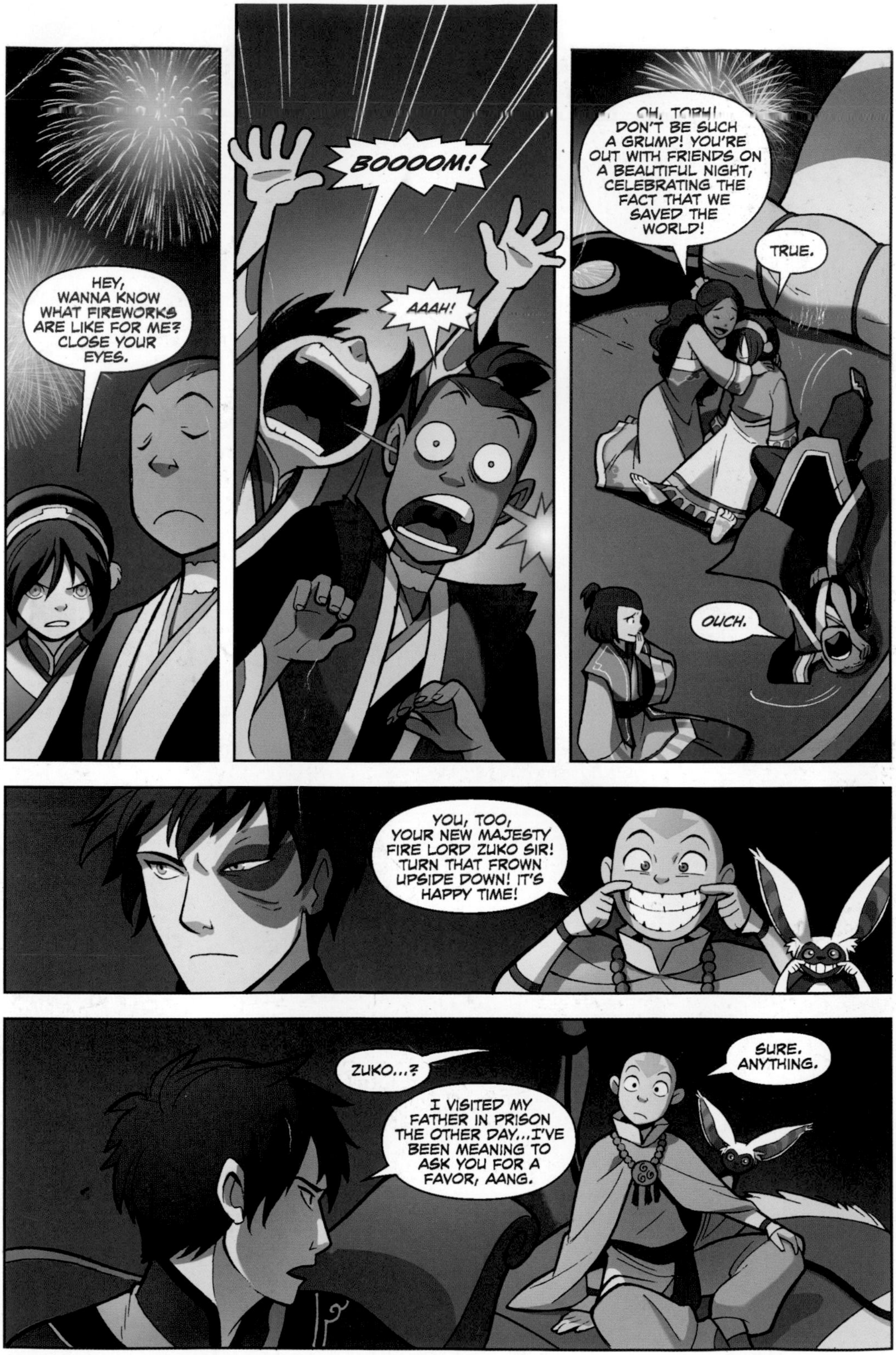
HEY, WANNA KNOW WHAT FIREWORKS ARE LIKE FOR ME? CLOSE YOUR EYES.
BOOOOM!
AAAH!
OH, TOPH! DON'T BE SUCH A GRUMP! YOU'RE OUT WITH FRIENDS ON A BEAUTIFUL NIGHT, CELEBRATING THE FACT THAT WE SAVED THE WORLD!
TRUE.
OUCH.
YOU, TOO, YOUR NEW MAJESTY FIRE LORD ZUKO SIR! TURN THAT FROWN UPSIDE DOWN! IT'S HAPPY TIME!
ZUKO...?
I VISITED MY FATHER IN PRISON THE OTHER DAY...I'VE BEEN MEANING TO ASK YOU FOR A FAVOR, AANG.
SURE. ANYTHING.

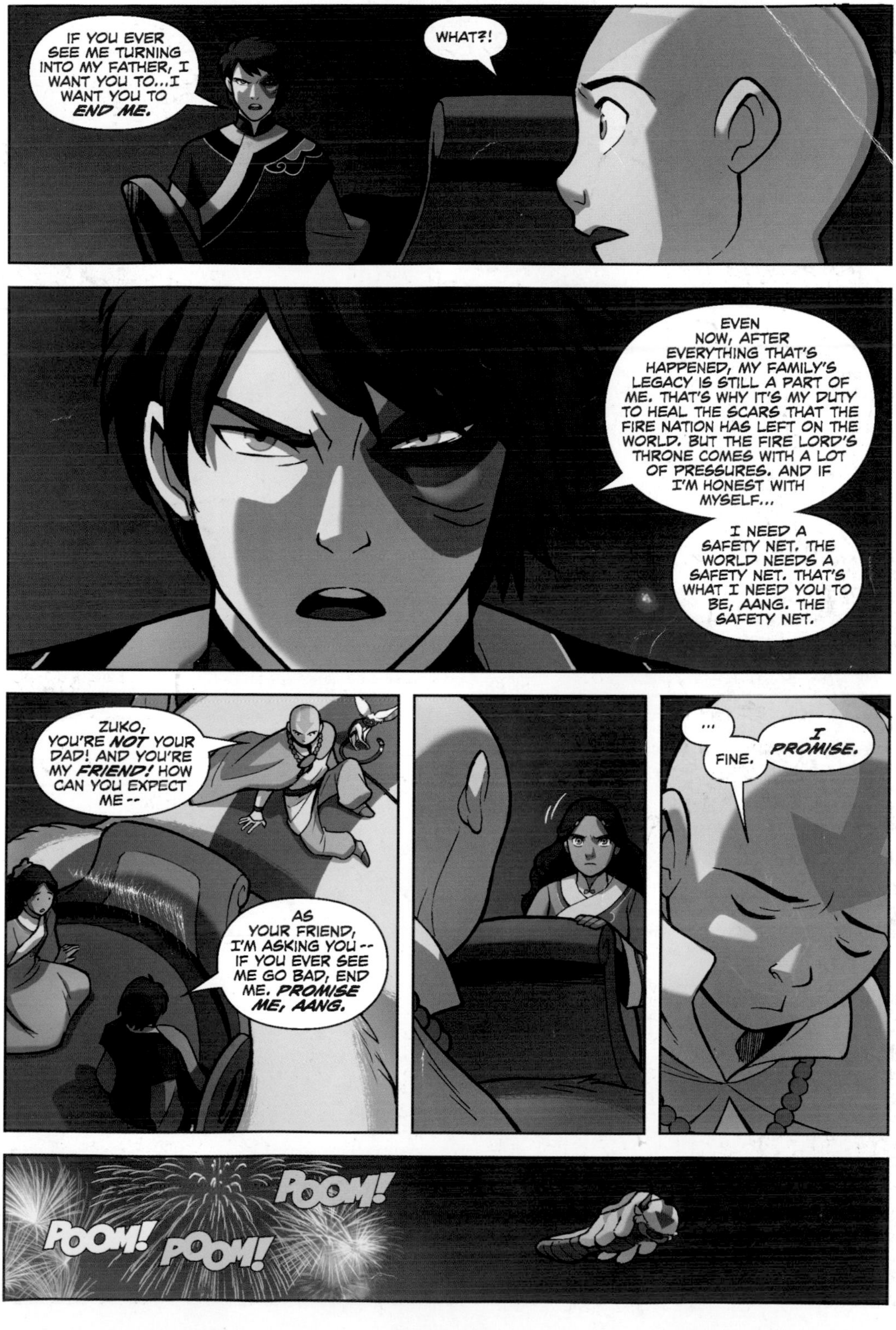
IF YOU EVER SEE ME TURNING INTO MY FATHER, I WANT YOU TO...I WANT YOU TO END ME.
WHAT?!
EVEN NOW, AFTER EVERYTHING THAT'S HAPPENED, MY FAMILY'S LEGACY IS STILL A PART OF ME. THAT'S WHY IT'S MY DUTY TO HEAL THE SCARS THAT THE FIRE NATION HAS LEFT ON THE WORLD. BUT THE FIRE LORD'S THRONE COMES WITH A LOT OF PRESSURES. AND IF I'M HONEST WITH MYSELF...
I NEED A SAFETY NET. THE WORLD NEEDS A SAFETY NET. THAT'S WHAT I NEED YOU TO BE, AANG. THE SAFETY NET.
ZUKO, YOU'RE NOT YOUR DAD! AND YOU'RE MY FRIEND! HOW CAN YOU EXPECT ME --
AS YOUR FRIEND, I'M ASKING YOU -- IF YOU EVER SEE ME GO BAD, END ME. PROMISE ME, AANG.
...
FINE.
I PROMISE.
POOM!
POOM!
POOM!

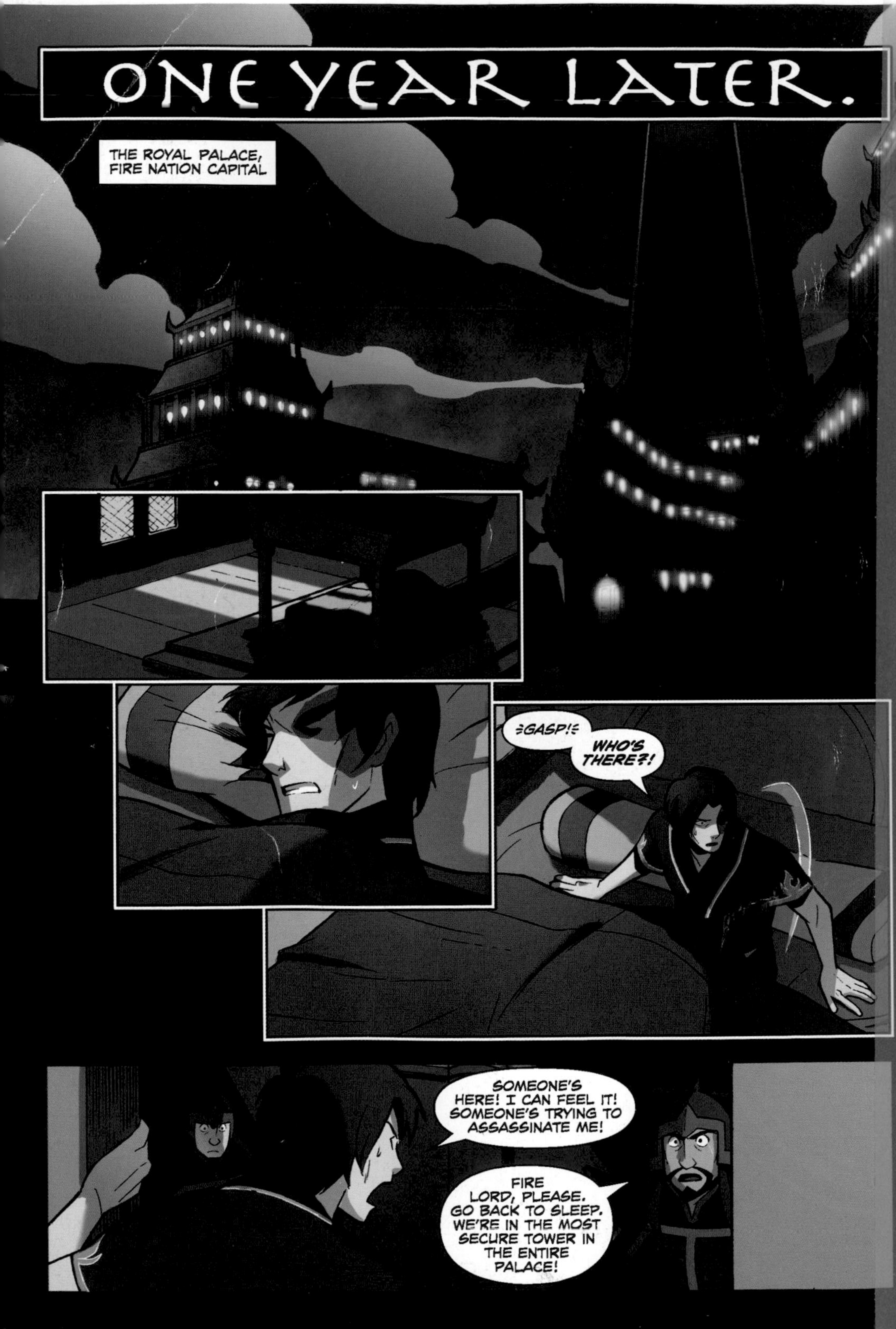
ONE YEAR LATER.
THE ROYAL PALACE, FIRE NATION CAPITAL
GASP!
WHO'S THERE?!
SOMEONE'S HERE! I CAN FEEL IT! SOMEONE'S TRYING TO ASSASSINATE ME!
FIRE LORD, PLEASE. GO BACK TO SLEEP. WE'RE IN THE MOST SECURE TOWER IN THE ENTIRE PALACE!

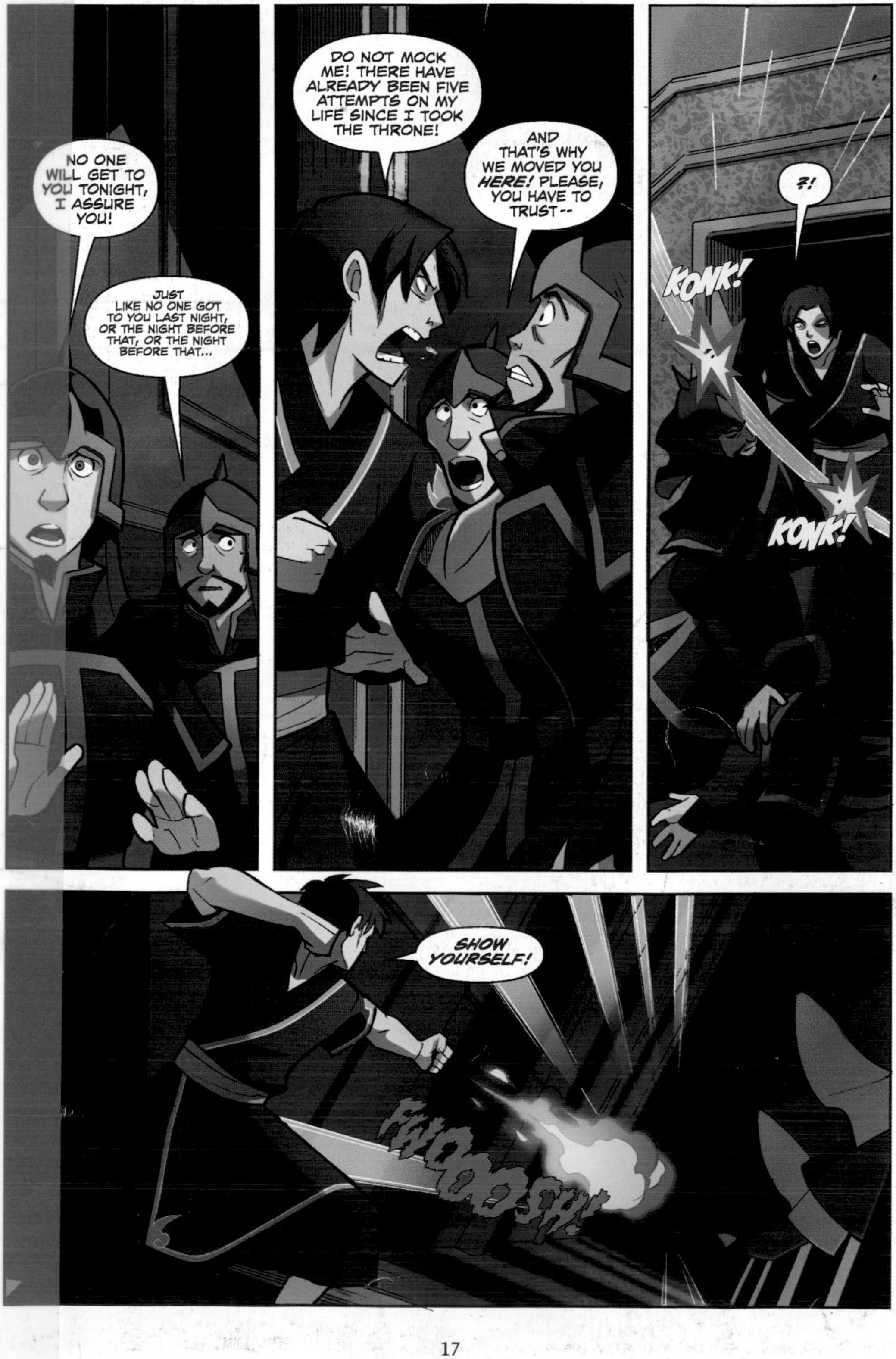
NO ONE WILL GET TO YOU TONIGHT, I ASSURE YOU!
JUST LIKE NO ONE GOT TO YOU LAST NIGHT, OR THE NIGHT BEFORE THAT, OR THE NIGHT BEFORE THAT...
DO NOT MOCK ME! THERE HAVE ALREADY BEEN FIVE ATTEMPTS ON MY LIFE SINCE I TOOK THE THRONE!
AND THAT'S WHY WE MOVED YOU HERE! PLEASE, YOU HAVE TO TRUST--
?!
KONK!
KONK!
SHOW YOURSELF!
FWOOOSH!

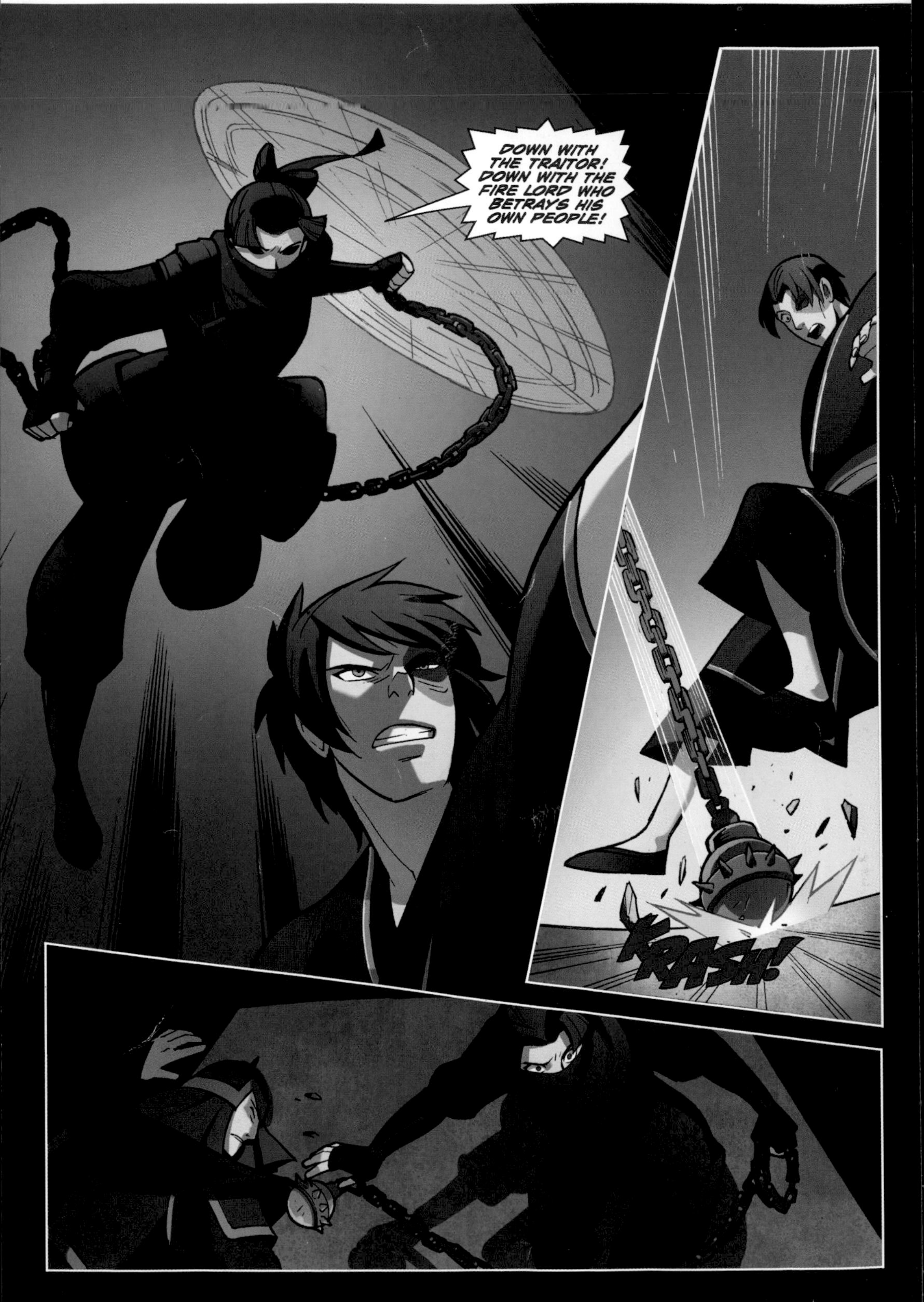
DOWN WITH THE TRAITOR! DOWN WITH THE FIRE LORD WHO BETRAYS HIS OWN PEOPLE!
KRASH!

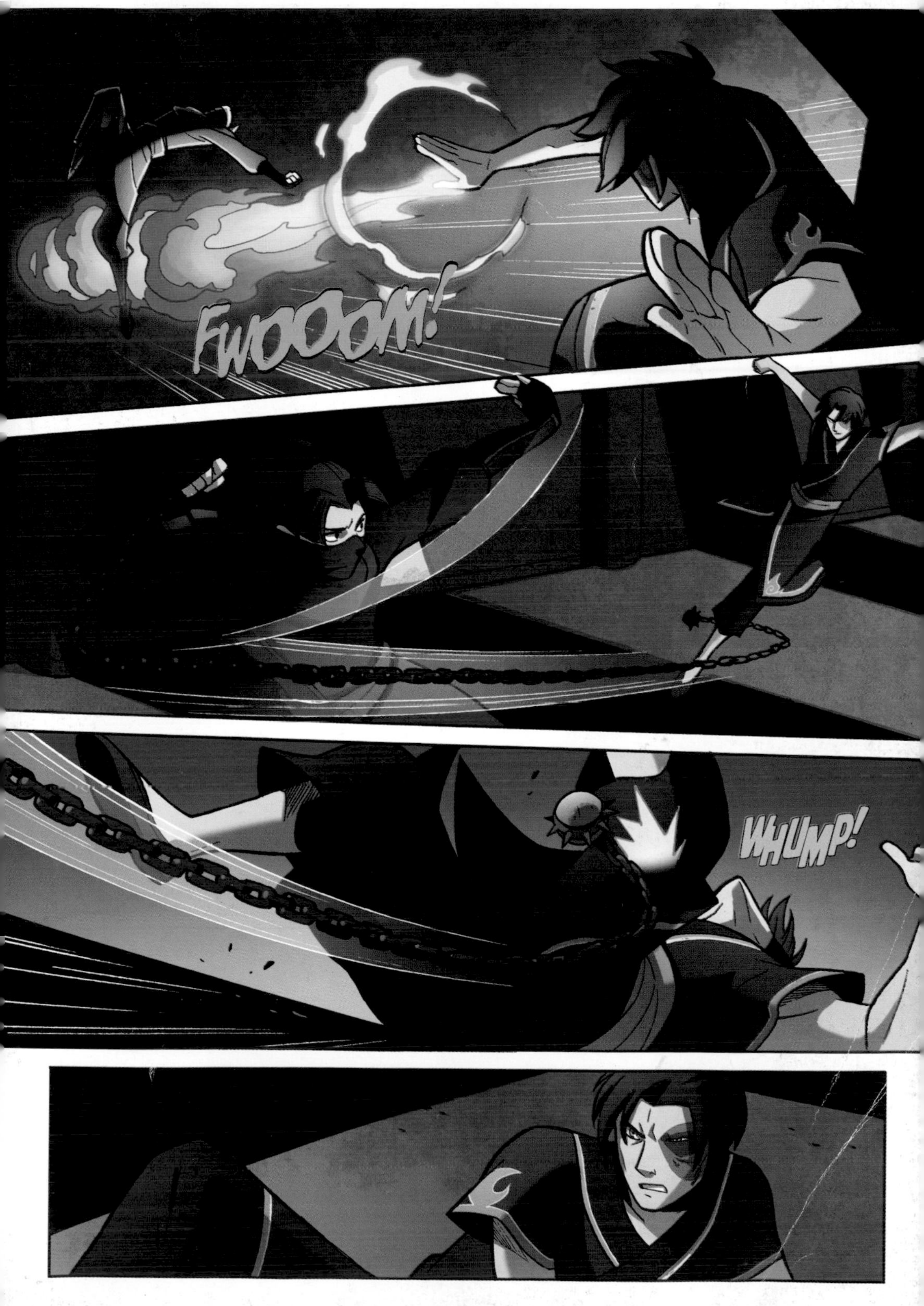
FWOOOM!
WHUMP!

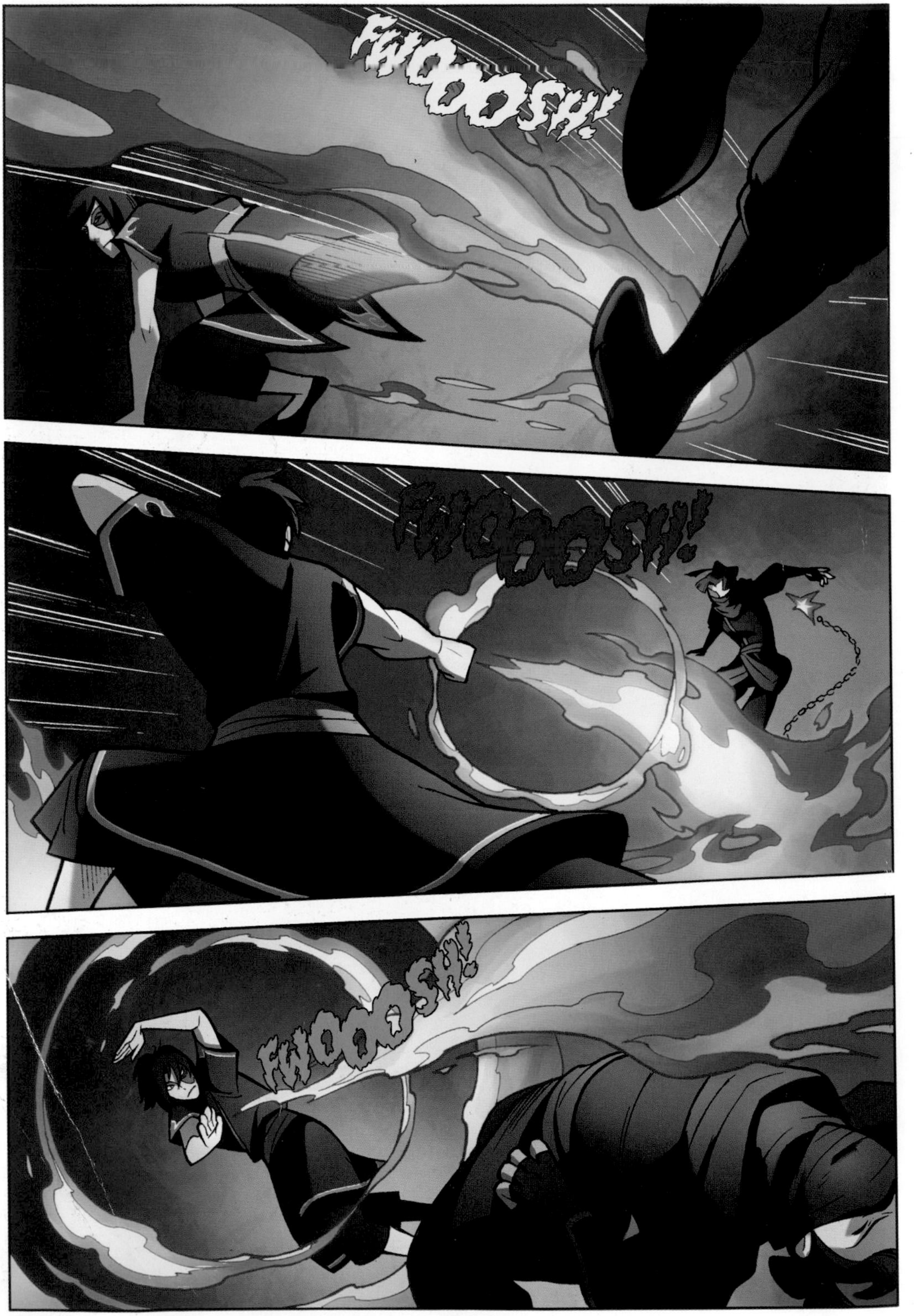
FWOOOSH!
FWOOOSH!
FWOOOSH!

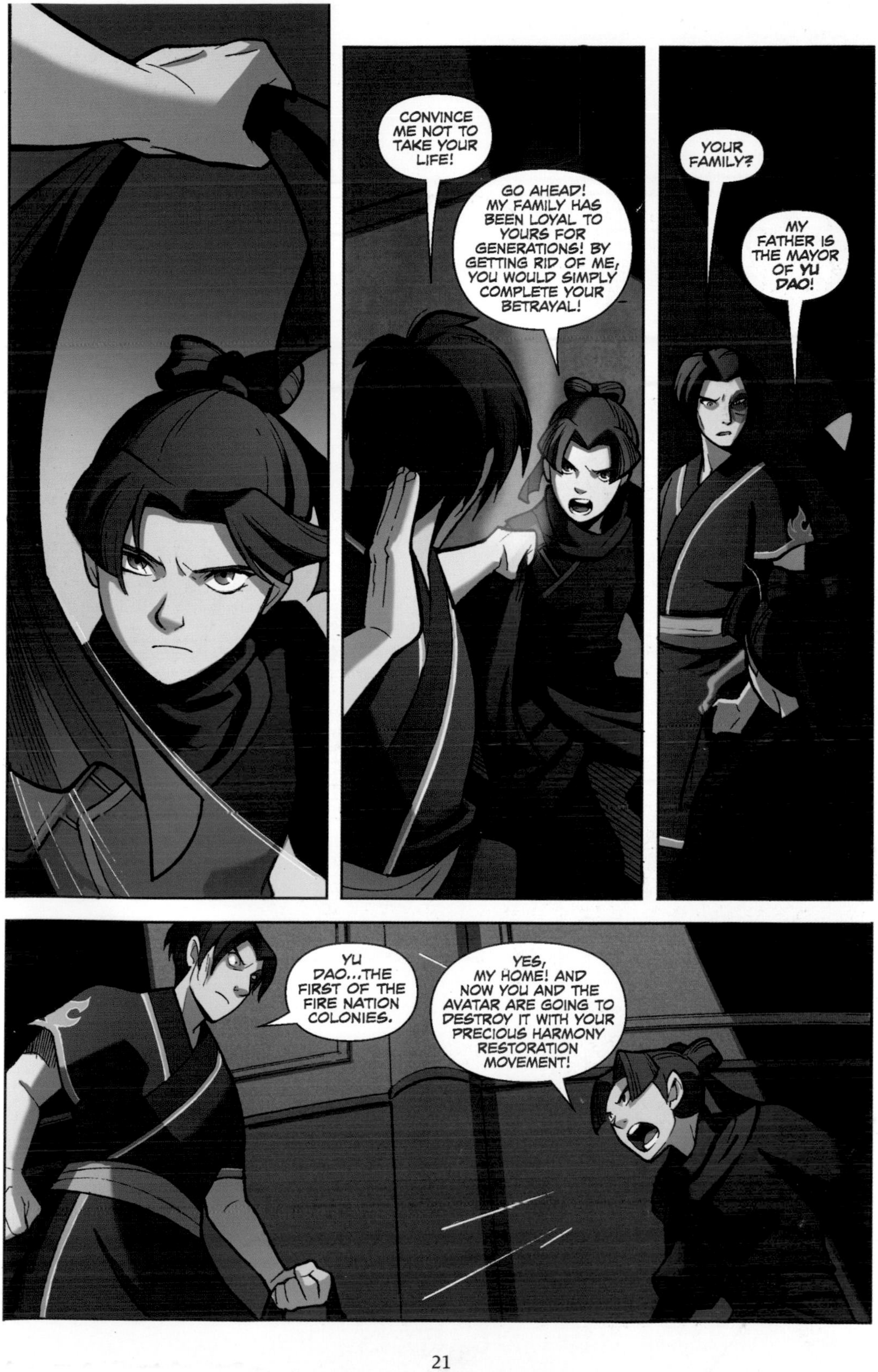
CONVINCE ME NOT TO TAKE YOUR LIFE!
GO AHEAD! MY FAMILY HAS BEEN LOYAL TO YOURS FOR GENERATIONS! BY GETTING RID OF ME, YOU WOULD SIMPLY COMPLETE YOUR BETRAYAL!
YOUR FAMILY?
MY FATHER IS THE MAYOR OF YU DAO!
YU DAO...THE FIRST OF THE FIRE NATION COLONIES.
YES, MY HOME! AND NOW YOU AND THE AVATAR ARE GOING TO DESTROY IT WITH YOUR PRECIOUS HARMONY RESTORATION MOVEMENT!

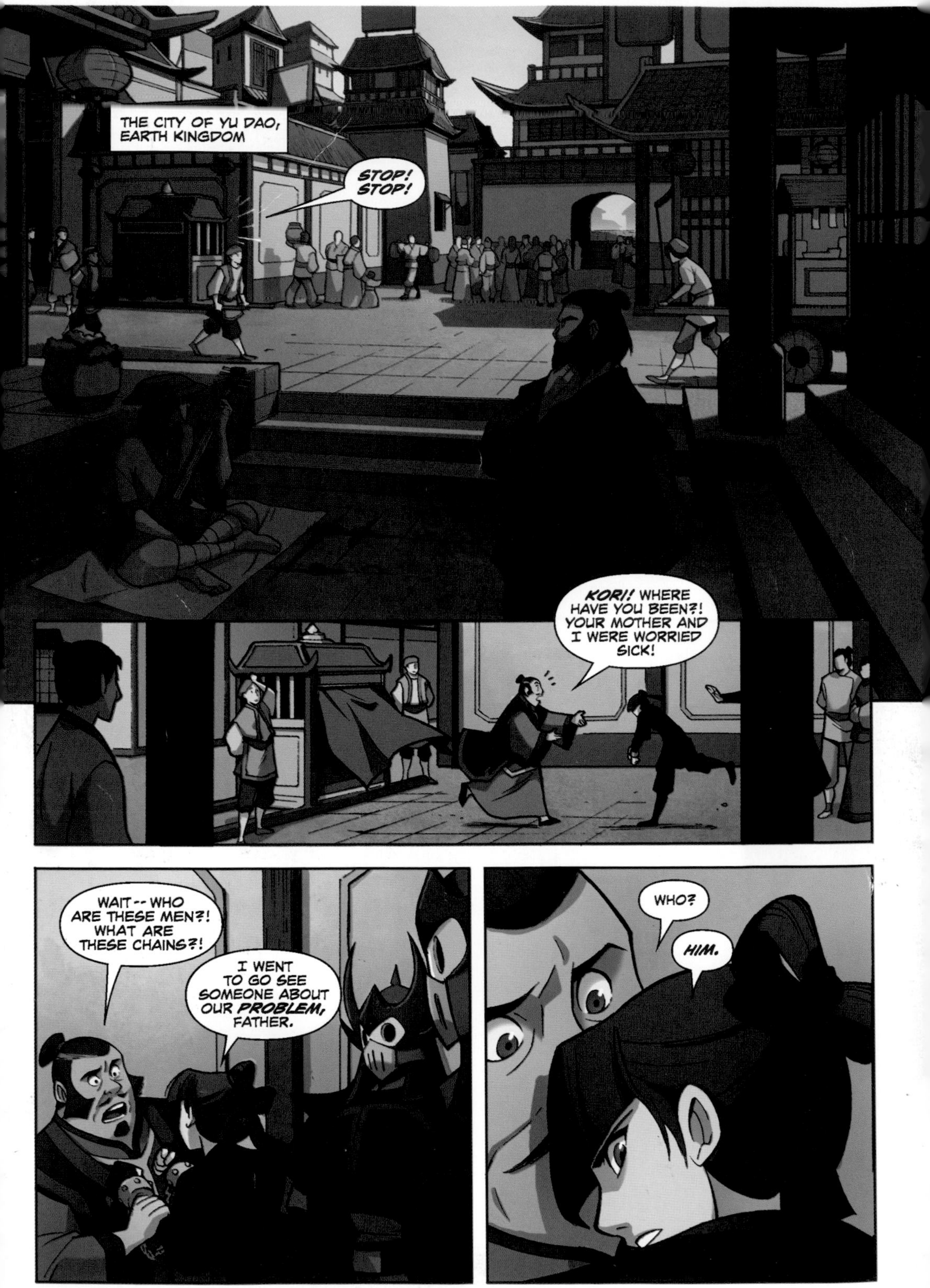
THE CITY OF YU DAO, EARTH KINGDOM
STOP! STOP!
KORI! WHERE HAVE YOU BEEN?! YOUR MOTHER AND I WERE WORRIED SICK!
WAIT-- WHO ARE THESE MEN?! WHAT ARE THESE CHAINS?!
I WENT TO GO SEE SOMEONE ABOUT OUR PROBLEM, FATHER.
WHO?
HIM.

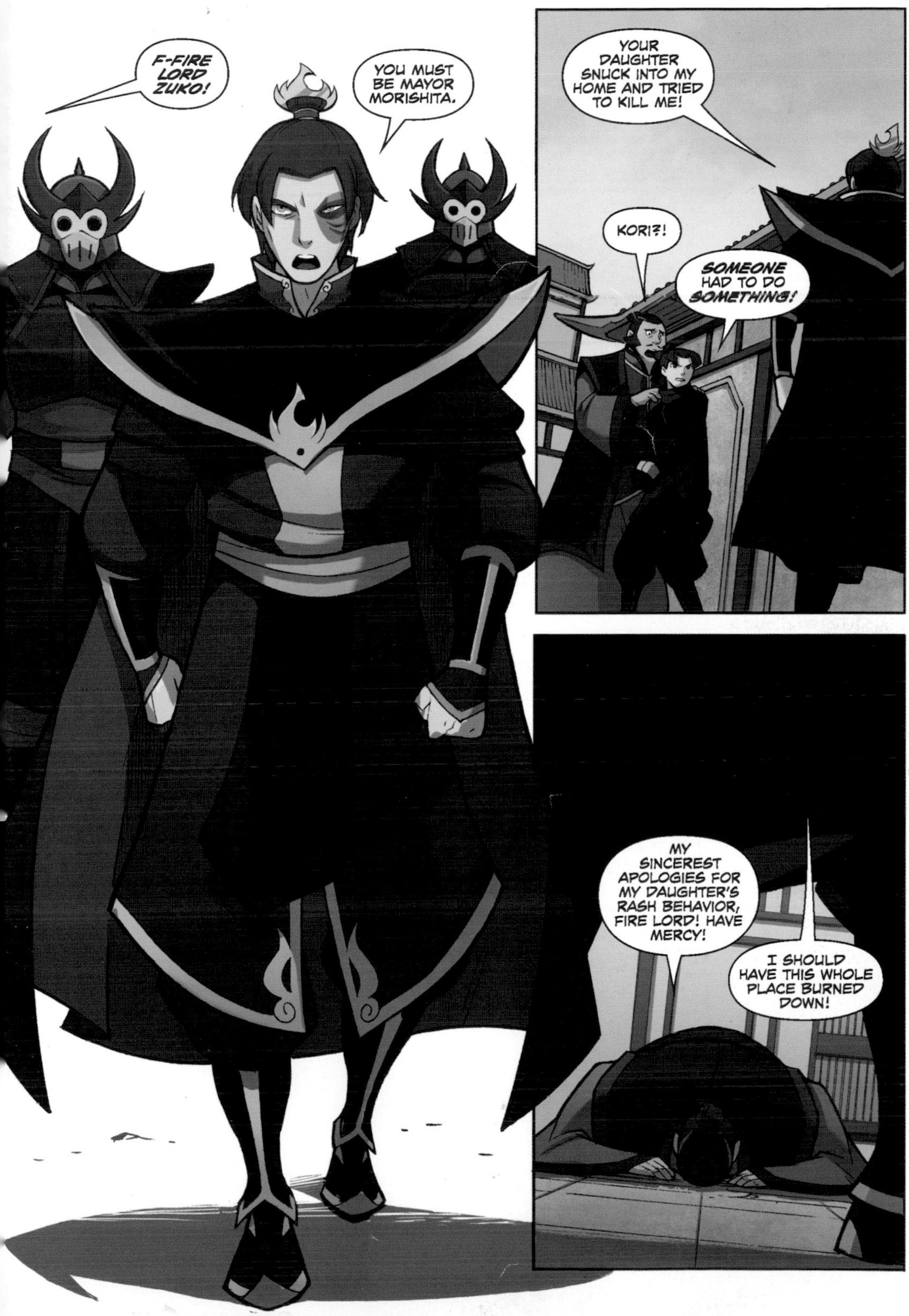
F-FIRE LORD ZUKO!
YOU MUST BE MAYOR MORISHITA.
YOUR DAUGHTER SNUCK INTO MY HOME AND TRIED TO KILL ME!
KORI?!
SOMEONE HAD TO DO SOMETHING!
MY SINCEREST APOLOGIES FOR MY DAUGHTER'S RASH BEHAVIOR, FIRE LORD! HAVE MERCY!
I SHOULD HAVE THIS WHOLE PLACE BURNED DOWN!

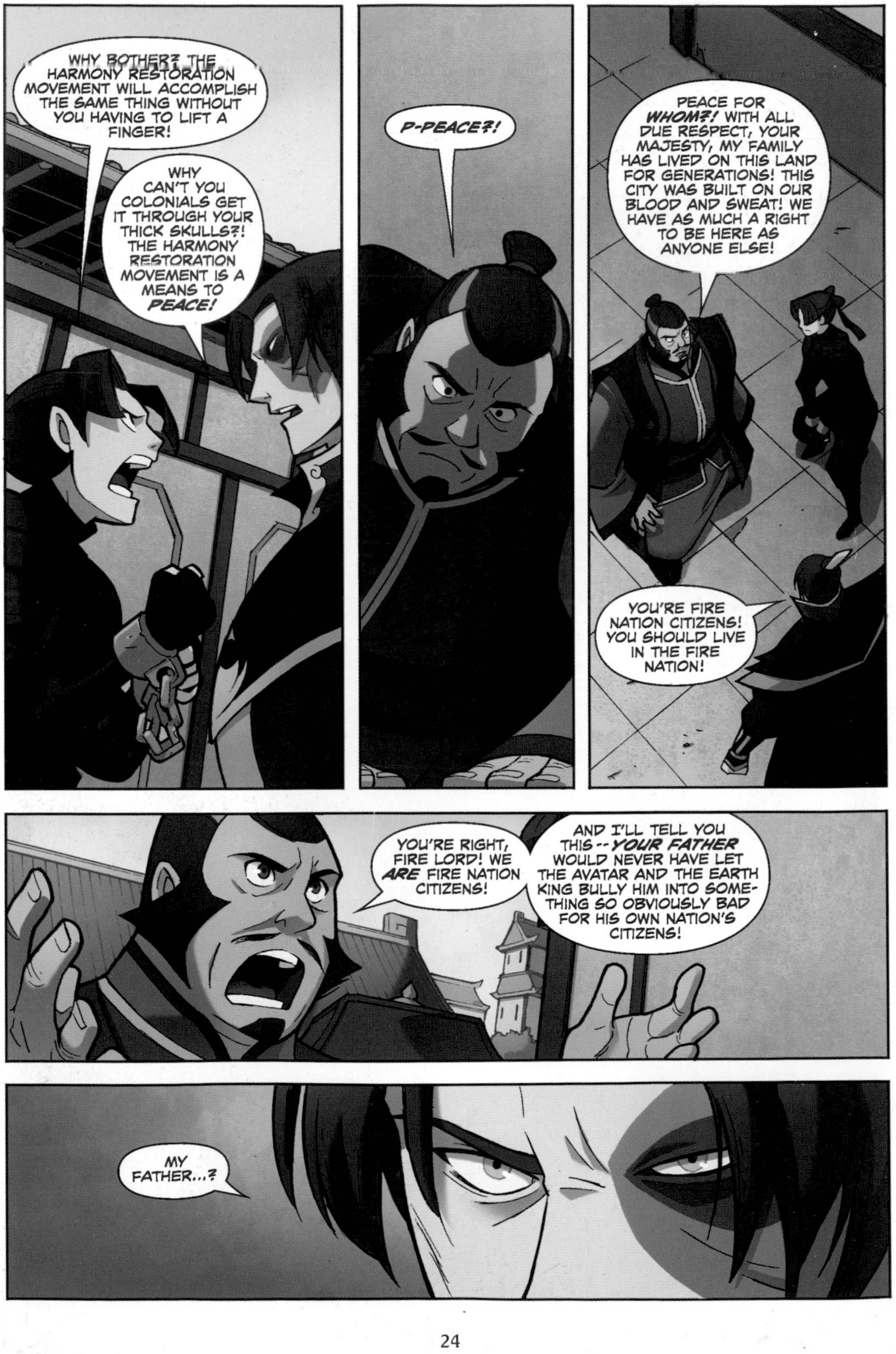
WHY BOTHER? THE HARMONY RESTORATION MOVEMENT WILL ACCOMPLISH THE SAME THING WITHOUT YOU HAVING TO LIFT A FINGER!
WHY CAN'T YOU COLONIALS GET IT THROUGH YOUR THICK SKULLS?! THE HARMONY RESTORATION MOVEMENT IS A MEANS TO PEACE!
P-PEACE?!
PEACE FOR WHOM?! WITH ALL DUE RESPECT, YOUR MAJESTY, MY FAMILY HAS LIVED ON THIS LAND FOR GENERATIONS! THIS CITY WAS BUILT ON OUR BLOOD AND SWEAT! WE HAVE AS MUCH A RIGHT TO BE HERE AS ANYONE ELSE!
YOU'RE FIRE NATION CITIZENS! YOU SHOULD LIVE IN THE FIRE NATION!
YOU'RE RIGHT, FIRE LORD! WE ARE FIRE NATION CITIZENS!
AND I'LL TELL YOU THIS--YOUR FATHER WOULD NEVER HAVE LET THE AVATAR AND THE EARTH KING BULLY HIM INTO SOMETHING SO OBVIOUSLY BAD FOR HIS OWN NATION'S CITIZENS!
MY FATHER...?

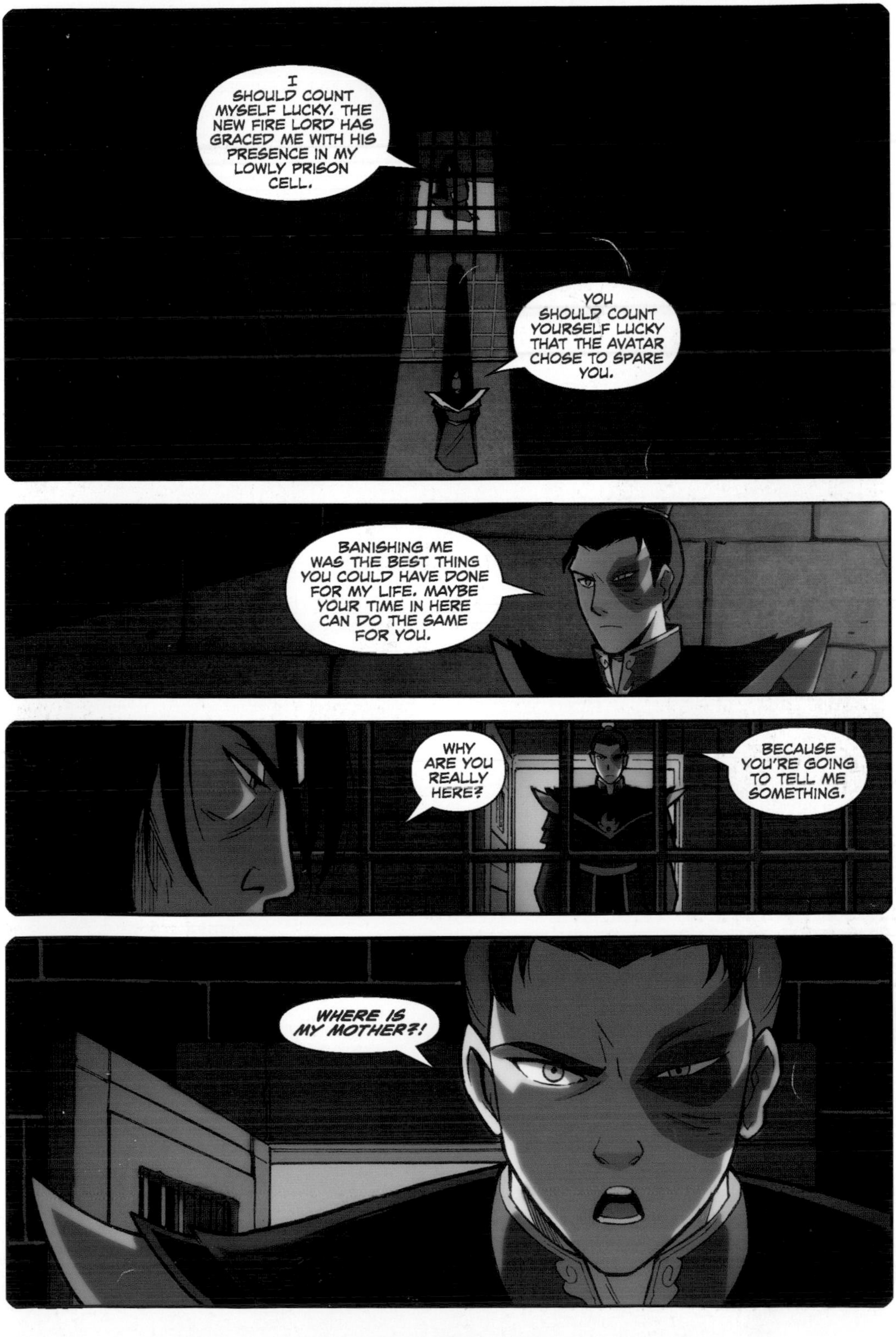
I SHOULD COUNT MYSELF LUCKY. THE NEW FIRE LORD HAS GRACED ME WITH HIS PRESENCE IN MY LOWLY PRISON CELL.
YOU SHOULD COUNT YOURSELF LUCKY THAT THE AVATAR CHOSE TO SPARE YOU.
BANISHING ME WAS THE BEST THING YOU COULD HAVE DONE FOR MY LIFE. MAYBE YOUR TIME IN HERE CAN DO THE SAME FOR YOU.
WHY ARE YOU REALLY HERE?
BECAUSE YOU'RE GOING TO TELL ME SOMETHING.
WHERE IS MY MOTHER?!

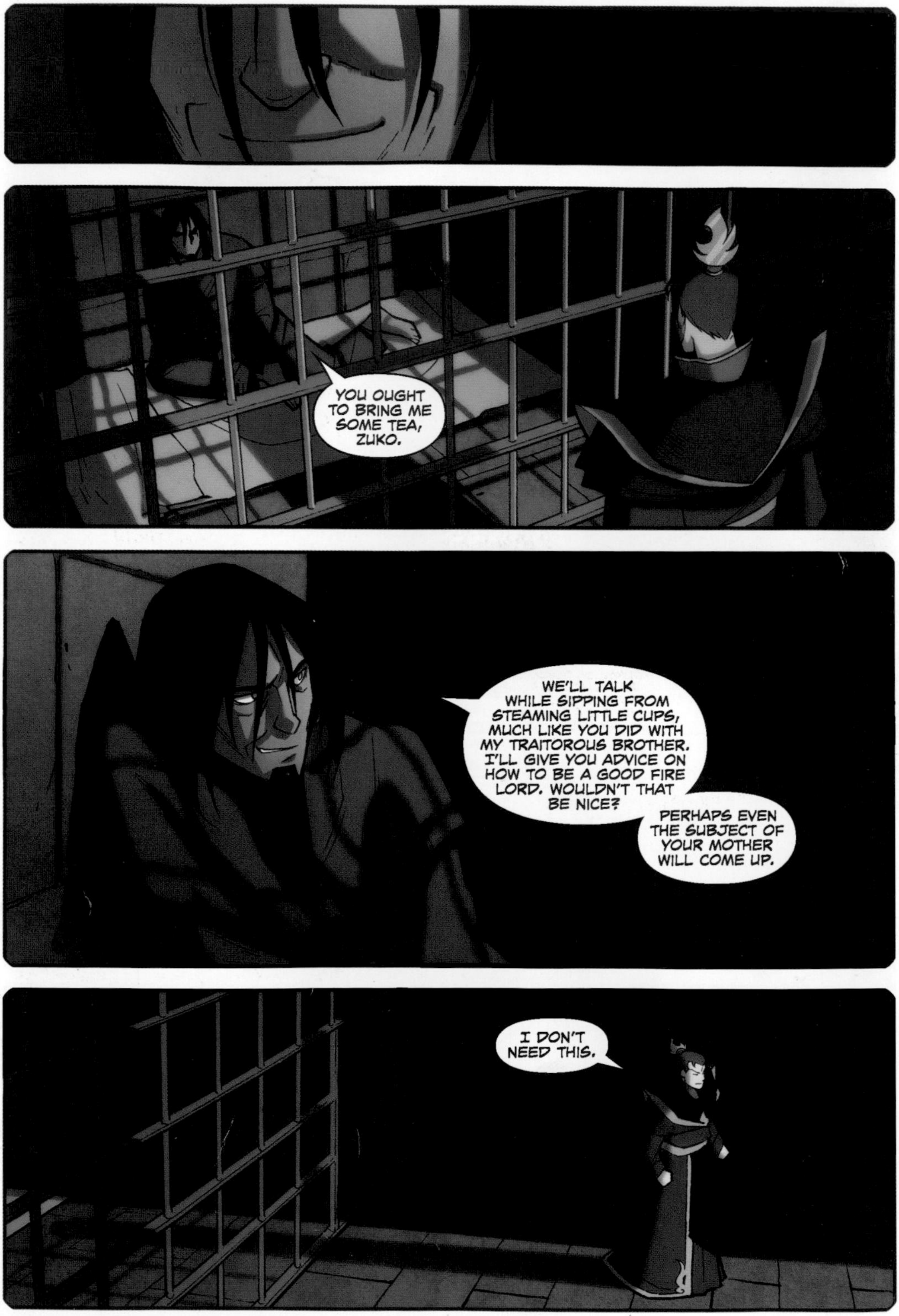
YOU OUGHT TO BRING ME SOME TEA, ZUKO.
WE'LL TALK WHILE SIPPING FROM STEAMING LITTLE CUPS, MUCH LIKE YOU DID WITH MY TRAITOROUS BROTHER. I'LL GIVE YOU ADVICE ON HOW TO BE A GOOD FIRE LORD. WOULDN'T THAT BE NICE?
PERHAPS EVEN THE SUBJECT OF YOUR MOTHER WILL COME UP.
I DON'T NEED THIS.

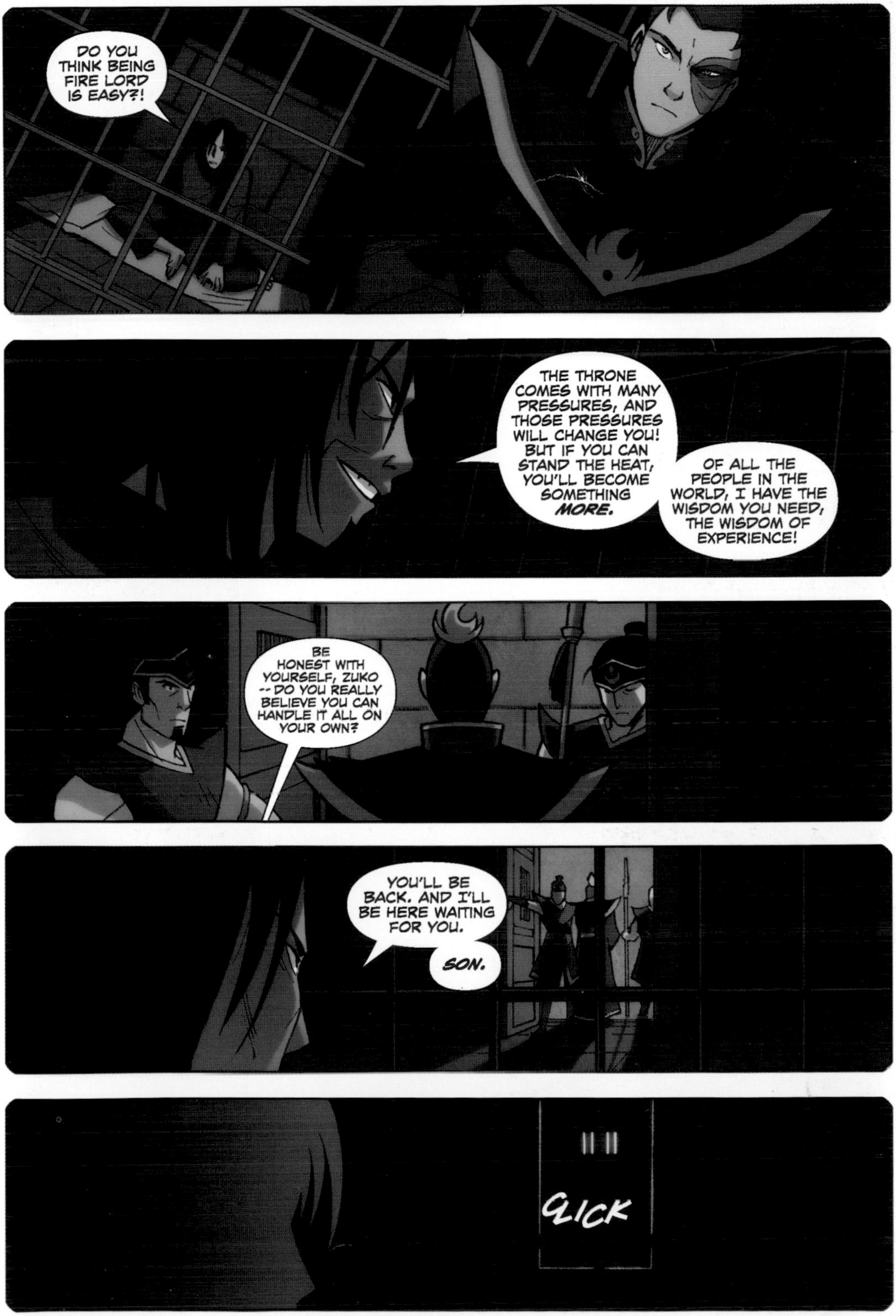
DO YOU THINK BEING FIRE LORD IS EASY?!
THE THRONE COMES WITH MANY PRESSURES, AND THOSE PRESSURES WILL CHANGE YOU! BUT IF YOU CAN STAND THE HEAT, YOU'LL BECOME SOMETHING *MORE.*
OF ALL THE PEOPLE IN THE WORLD, I HAVE THE WISDOM YOU NEED, THE WISDOM OF EXPERIENCE!
BE HONEST WITH YOURSELF, ZUKO -- DO YOU REALLY BELIEVE YOU CAN HANDLE IT ALL ON YOUR OWN?
YOU'LL BE BACK. AND I'LL BE HERE WAITING FOR YOU.
SON.
CLICK

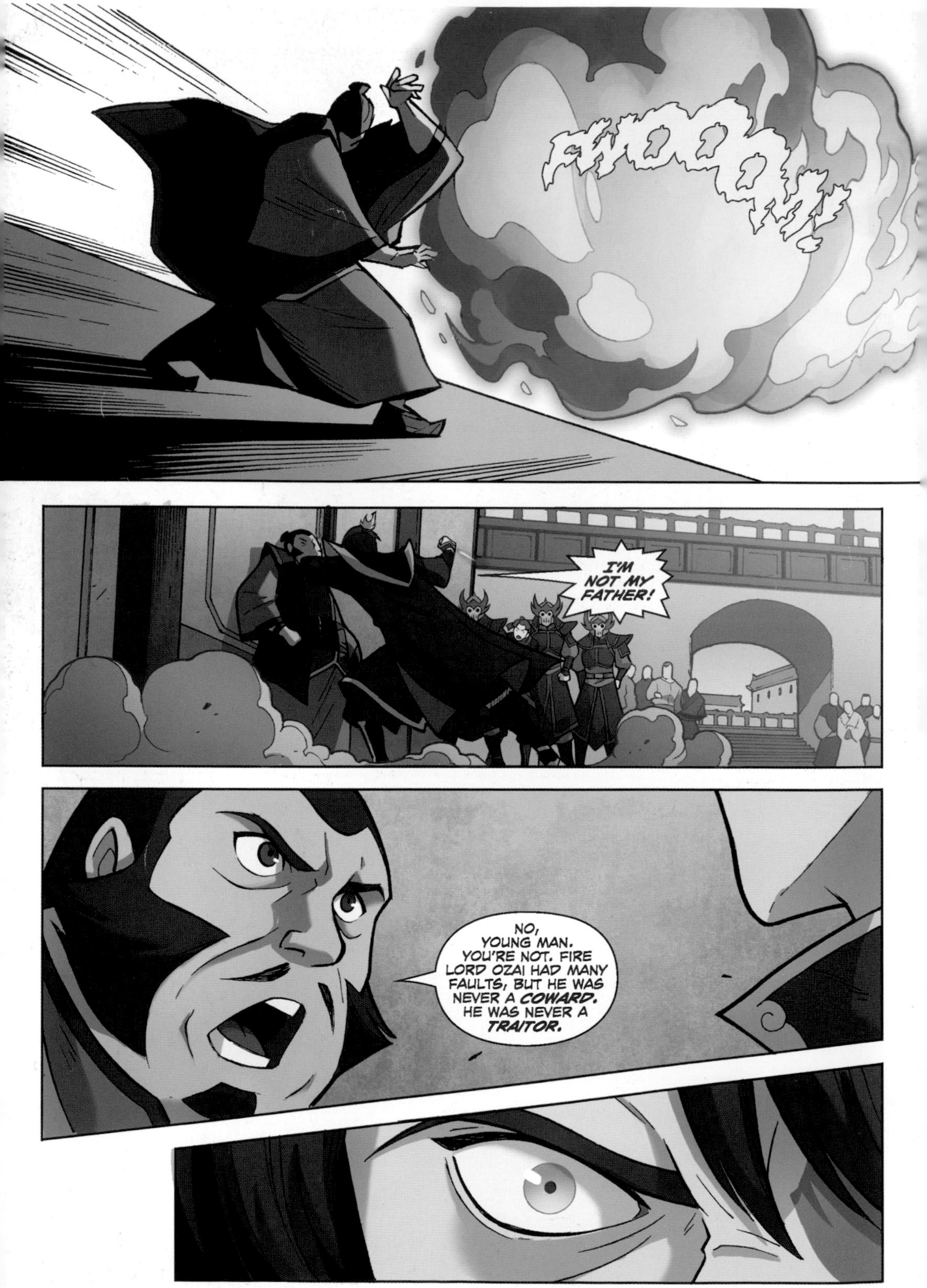
FWOOOM!
I'M NOT MY FATHER!
NO, YOUNG MAN. YOU'RE NOT. FIRE LORD OZAI HAD MANY FAULTS, BUT HE WAS NEVER A COWARD. HE WAS NEVER A TRAITOR.

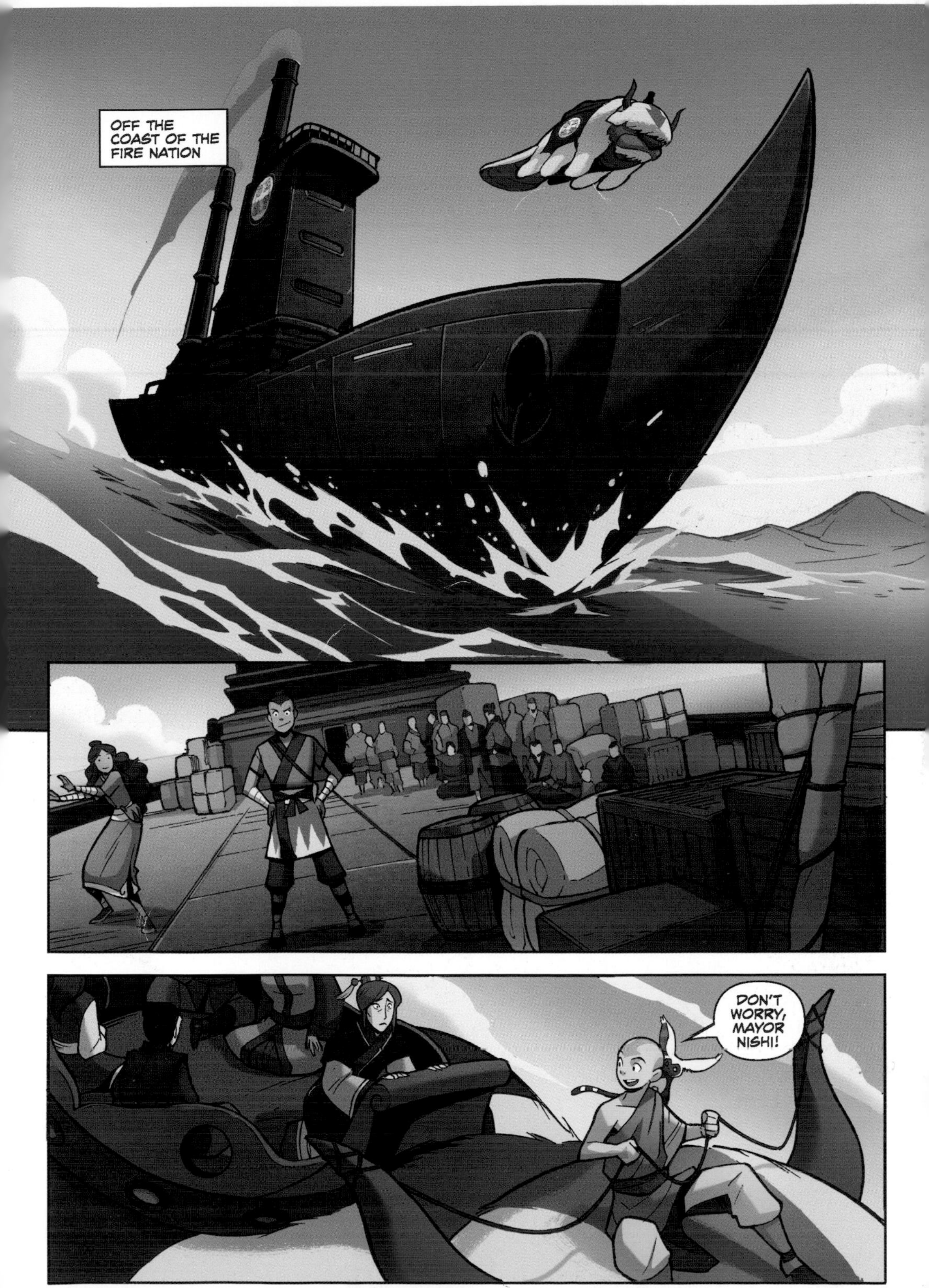
OFF THE COAST OF THE FIRE NATION
DON'T WORRY, MAYOR NISHI!

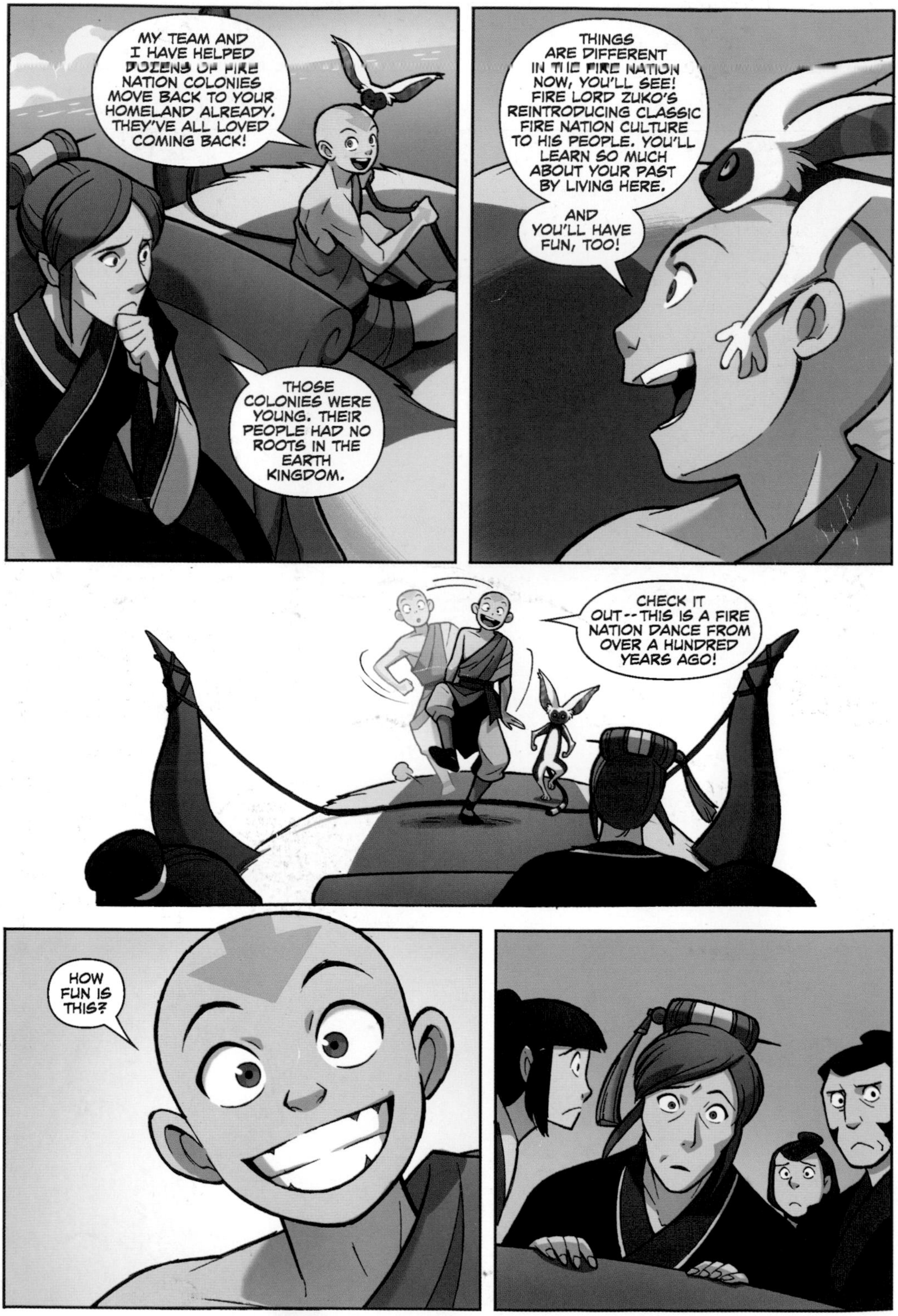
MY TEAM AND I HAVE HELPED DOZENS OF FIRE NATION COLONIES MOVE BACK TO YOUR HOMELAND ALREADY. THEY'VE ALL LOVED COMING BACK!
THOSE COLONIES WERE YOUNG. THEIR PEOPLE HAD NO ROOTS IN THE EARTH KINGDOM.
THINGS ARE DIFFERENT IN THE FIRE NATION NOW, YOU'LL SEE! FIRE LORD ZUKO'S REINTRODUCING CLASSIC FIRE NATION CULTURE TO HIS PEOPLE. YOU'LL LEARN SO MUCH ABOUT YOUR PAST BY LIVING HERE.
AND YOU'LL HAVE FUN, TOO!
CHECK IT OUT--THIS IS A FIRE NATION DANCE FROM OVER A HUNDRED YEARS AGO!
HOW FUN IS THIS?

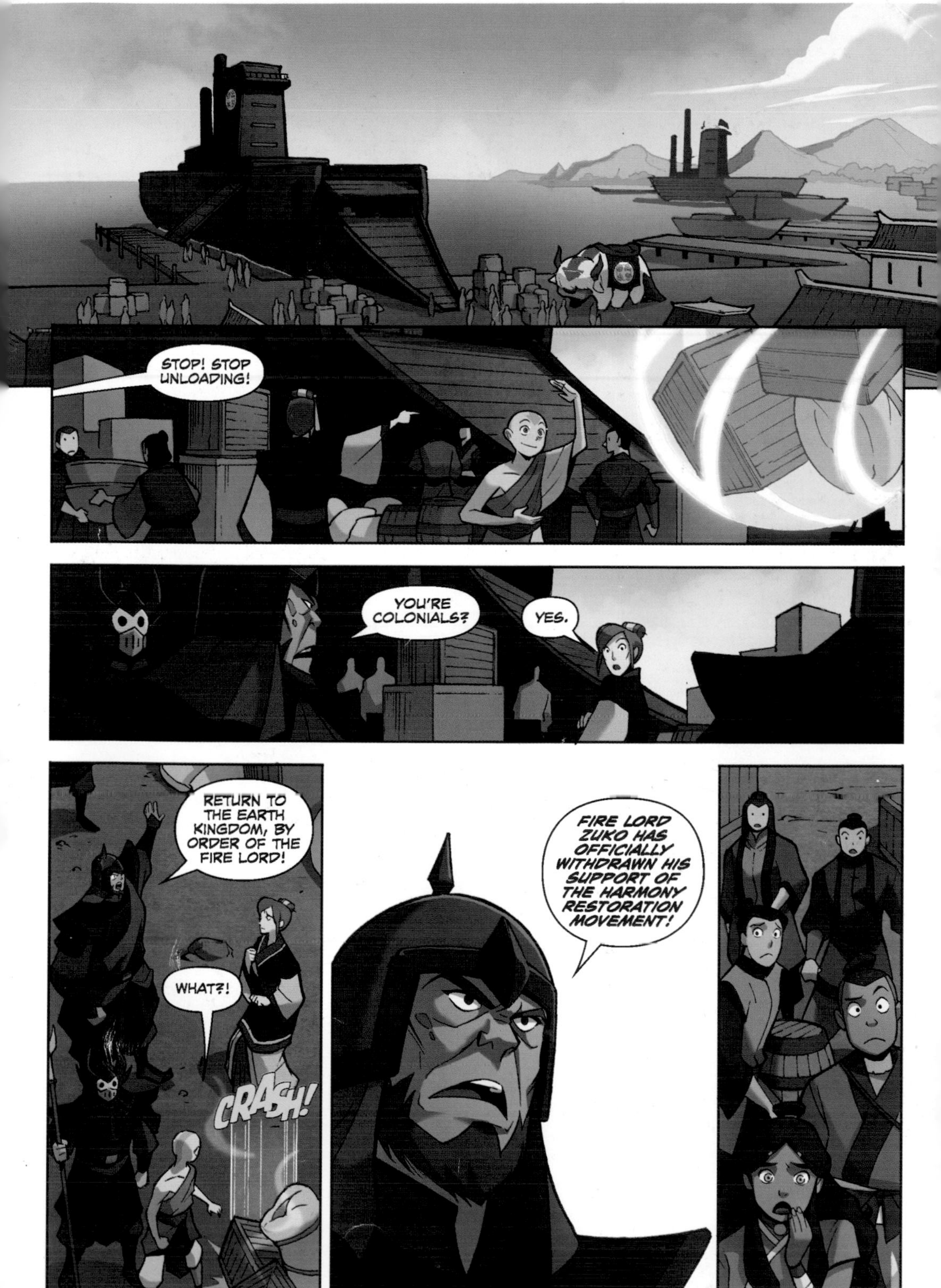
STOP! STOP UNLOADING!
YOU'RE COLONIALS?
YES.
RETURN TO THE EARTH KINGDOM, BY ORDER OF THE FIRE LORD!
WHAT?!
CRASH!
FIRE LORD ZUKO HAS OFFICIALLY WITHDRAWN HIS SUPPORT OF THE HARMONY RESTORATION MOVEMENT!

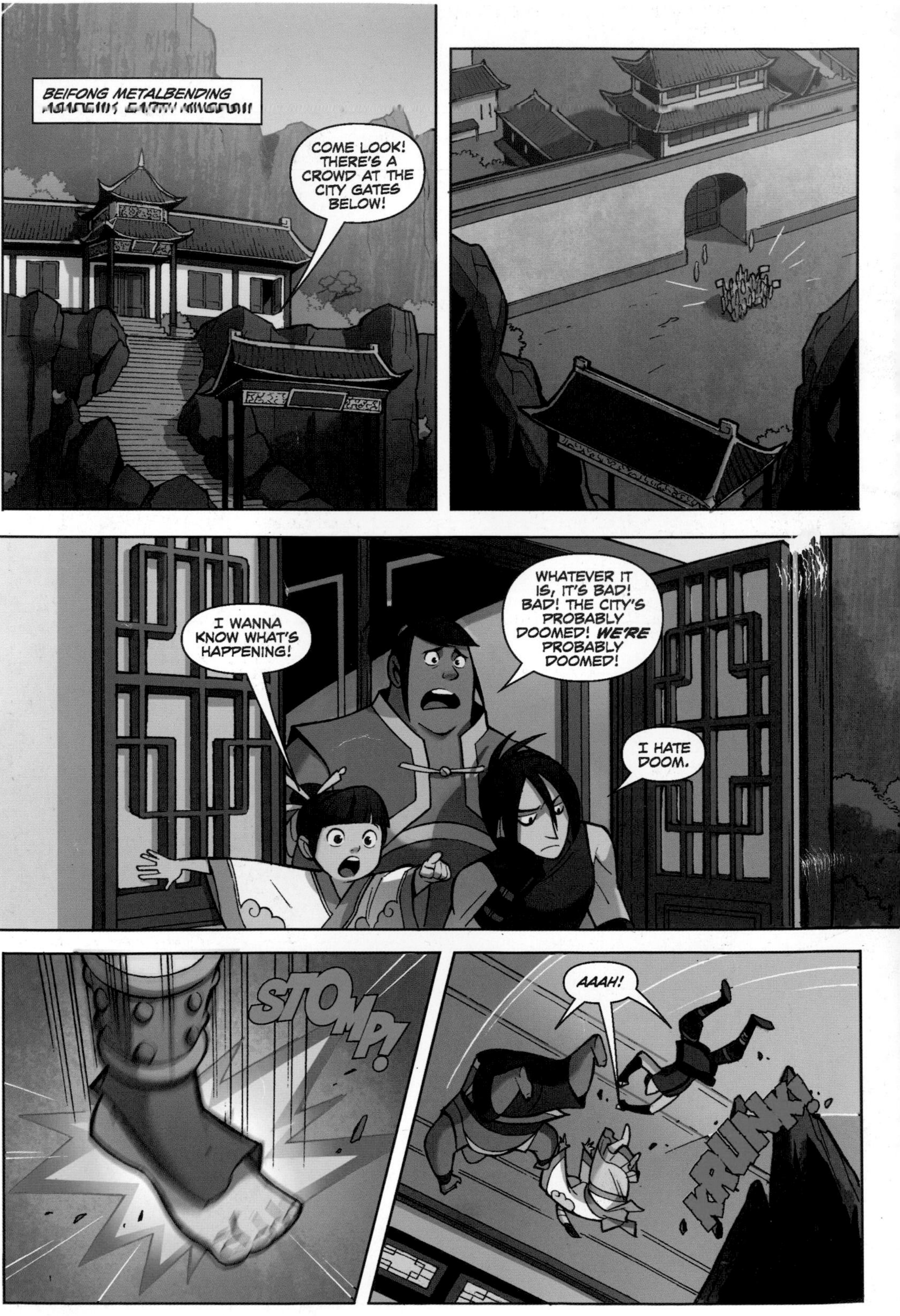
BEIFONG METALBENDING
COME LOOK! THERE'S A CROWD AT THE CITY GATES BELOW!
I WANNA KNOW WHAT'S HAPPENING!
WHATEVER IT IS, IT'S BAD! BAD! THE CITY'S PROBABLY DOOMED! *WE'RE* PROBABLY DOOMED!
I HATE DOOM.
STOMP!
AAAH!
KRUNK!

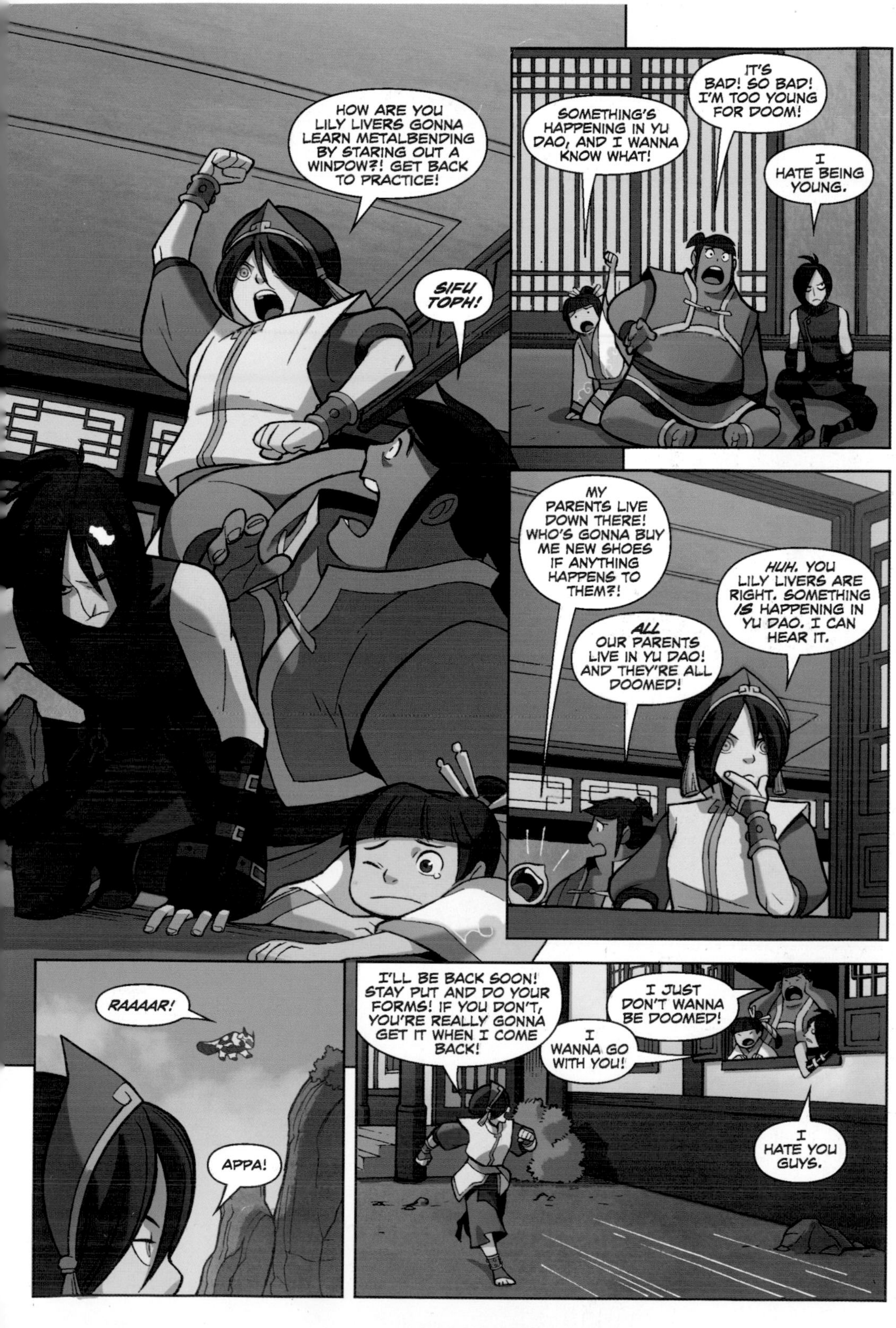

HOW ARE YOU LILY LIVERS GONNA LEARN METALBENDING BY STARING OUT A WINDOW?! GET BACK TO PRACTICE!
SIFU TOPH!
SOMETHING'S HAPPENING IN YU DAO, AND I WANNA KNOW WHAT!
IT'S BAD! SO BAD! I'M TOO YOUNG FOR DOOM!
I HATE BEING YOUNG.
MY PARENTS LIVE DOWN THERE! WHO'S GONNA BUY ME NEW SHOES IF ANYTHING HAPPENS TO THEM?!
ALL OUR PARENTS LIVE IN YU DAO! AND THEY'RE ALL DOOMED!
HUH. YOU LILY LIVERS ARE RIGHT. SOMETHING IS HAPPENING IN YU DAO. I CAN HEAR IT.
RAAAAR!
APPA!
I'LL BE BACK SOON! STAY PUT AND DO YOUR FORMS! IF YOU DON'T, YOU'RE REALLY GONNA GET IT WHEN I COME BACK!
I WANNA GO WITH YOU!
I JUST DON'T WANNA BE DOOMED!
I HATE YOU GUYS.

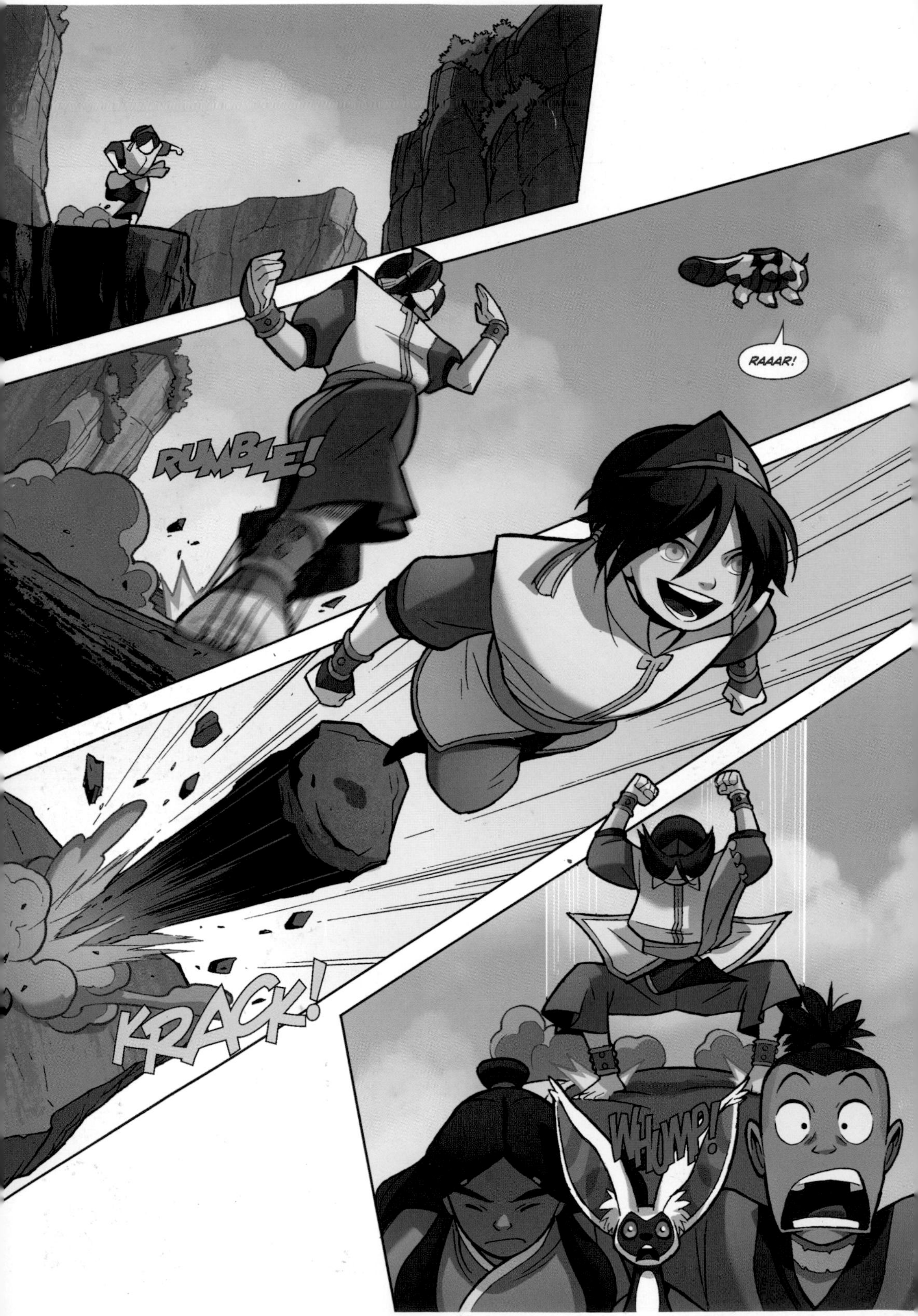
RAAAR!
RUMBLE!
KRACK!
WHUMP!

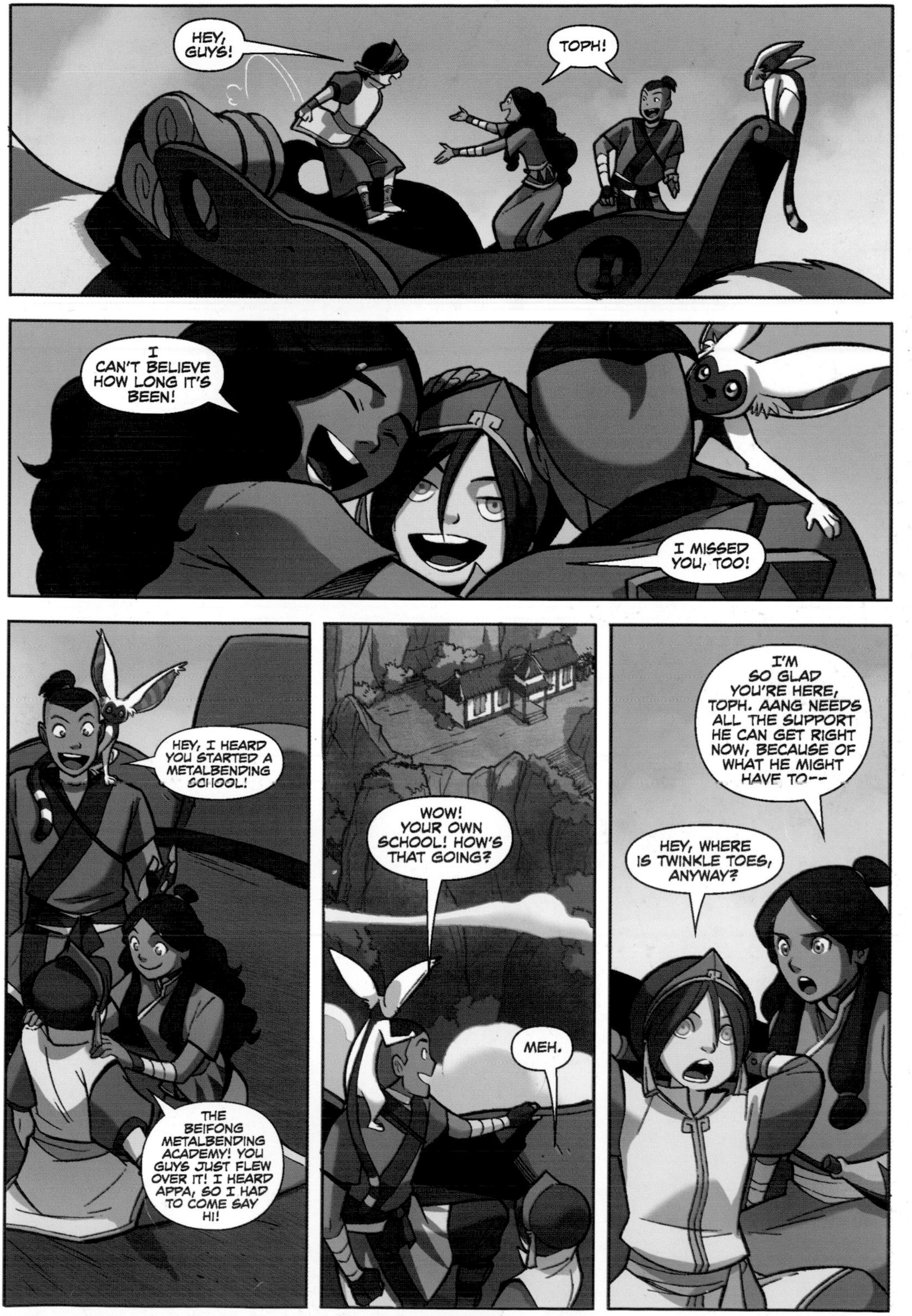
HEY, GUYS!
TOPH!
I CAN'T BELIEVE HOW LONG IT'S BEEN!
I MISSED YOU, TOO!
HEY, I HEARD YOU STARTED A METALBENDING SCHOOL!
THE BEIFONG METALBENDING ACADEMY! YOU GUYS JUST FLEW OVER IT! I HEARD APPA, SO I HAD TO COME SAY HI!
WOW! YOUR OWN SCHOOL! HOW'S THAT GOING?
MEH.
I'M SO GLAD YOU'RE HERE, TOPH. AANG NEEDS ALL THE SUPPORT HE CAN GET RIGHT NOW, BECAUSE OF WHAT HE MIGHT HAVE TO--
HEY, WHERE IS TWINKLE TOES, ANYWAY?

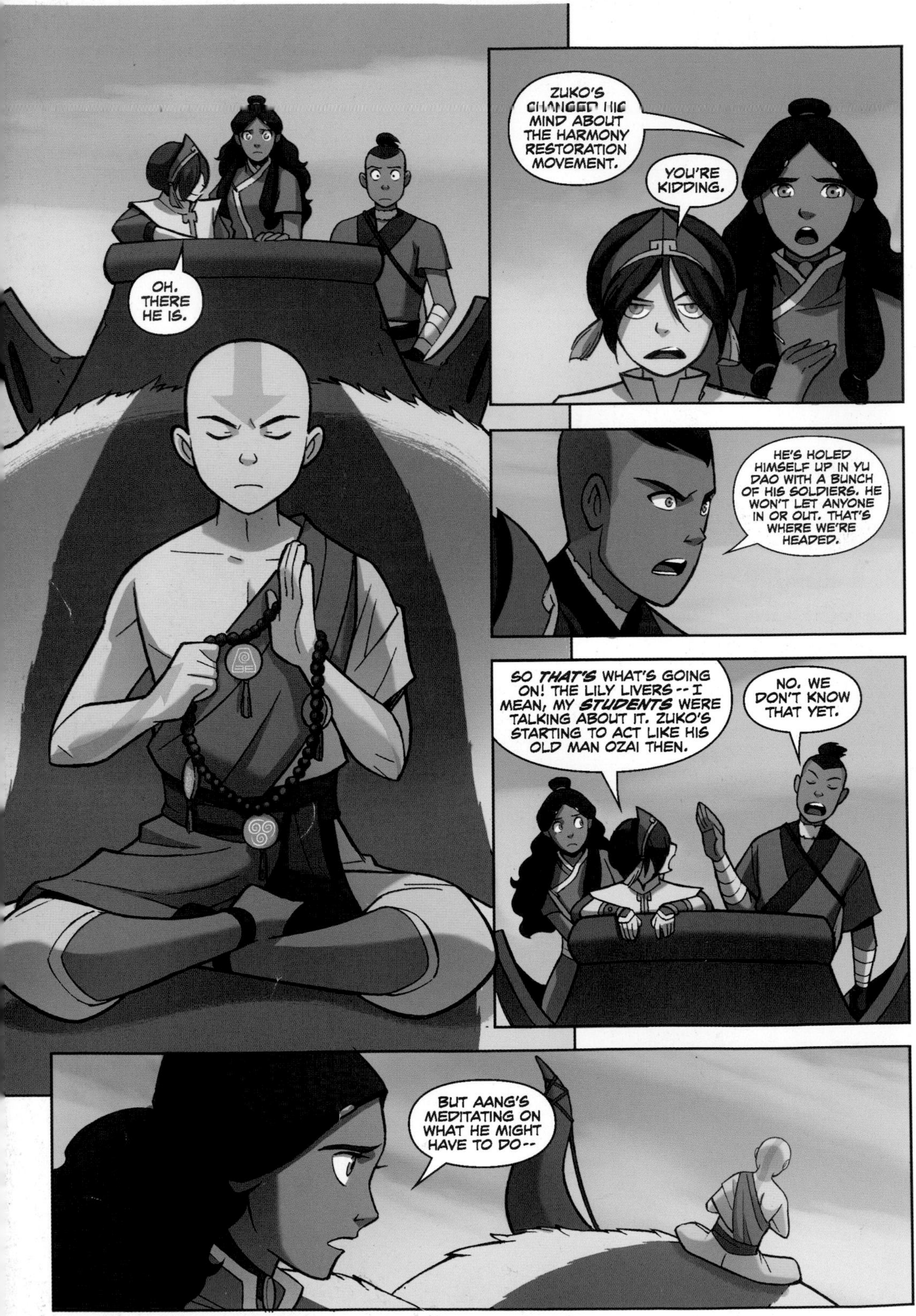
OH. THERE HE IS.
ZUKO'S CHANGED HIS MIND ABOUT THE HARMONY RESTORATION MOVEMENT.
YOU'RE KIDDING.
HE'S HOLED HIMSELF UP IN YU DAO WITH A BUNCH OF HIS SOLDIERS. HE WON'T LET ANYONE IN OR OUT. THAT'S WHERE WE'RE HEADED.
SO *THAT'S* WHAT'S GOING ON! THE LILY LIVERS -- I MEAN, MY *STUDENTS* WERE TALKING ABOUT IT. ZUKO'S STARTING TO ACT LIKE HIS OLD MAN OZAI THEN.
NO. WE DON'T KNOW THAT YET.
BUT AANG'S MEDITATING ON WHAT HE MIGHT HAVE TO DO--

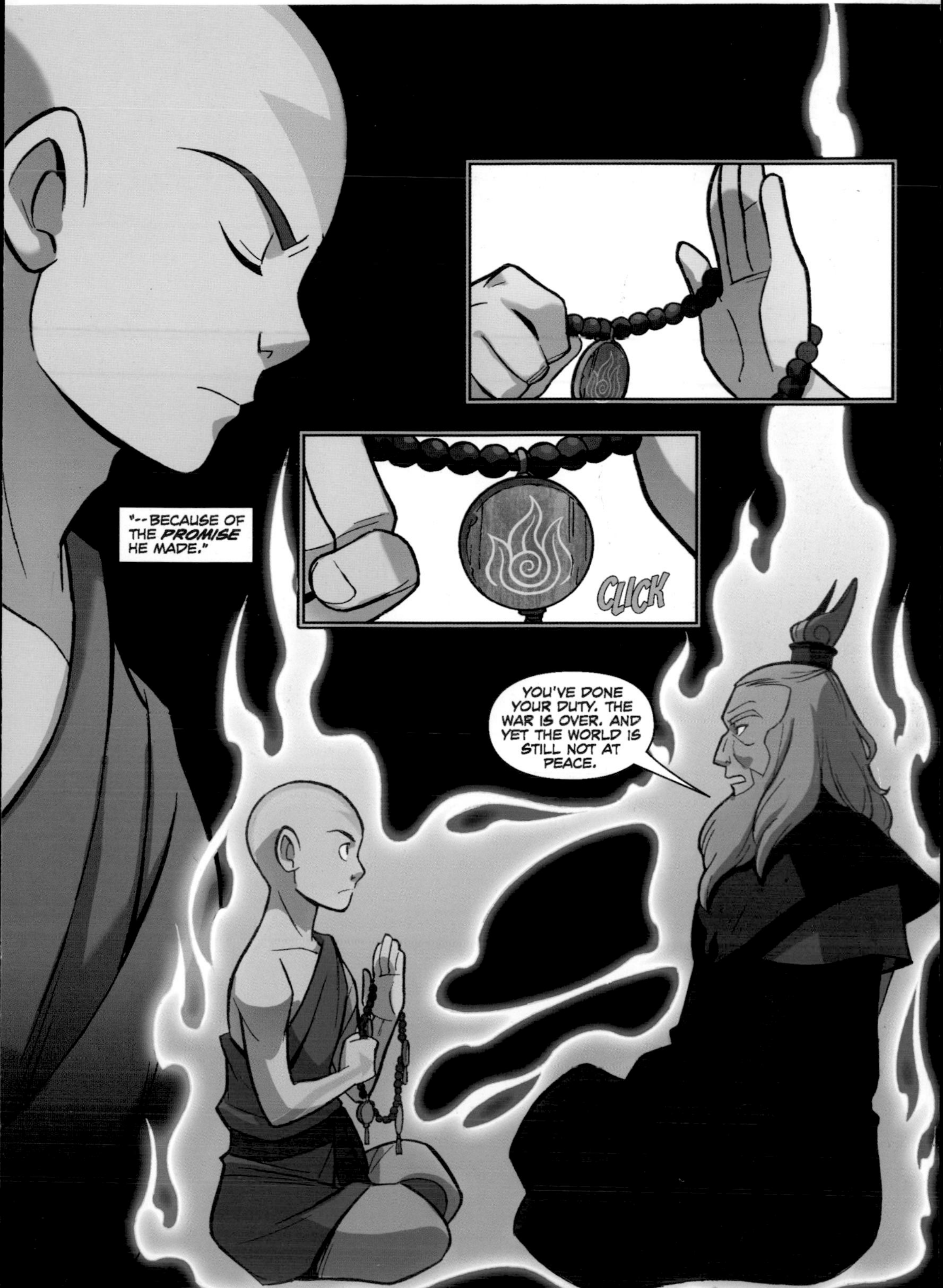
"--BECAUSE OF THE PROMISE HE MADE."
CLICK
YOU'VE DONE YOUR DUTY. THE WAR IS OVER. AND YET THE WORLD IS STILL NOT AT PEACE.

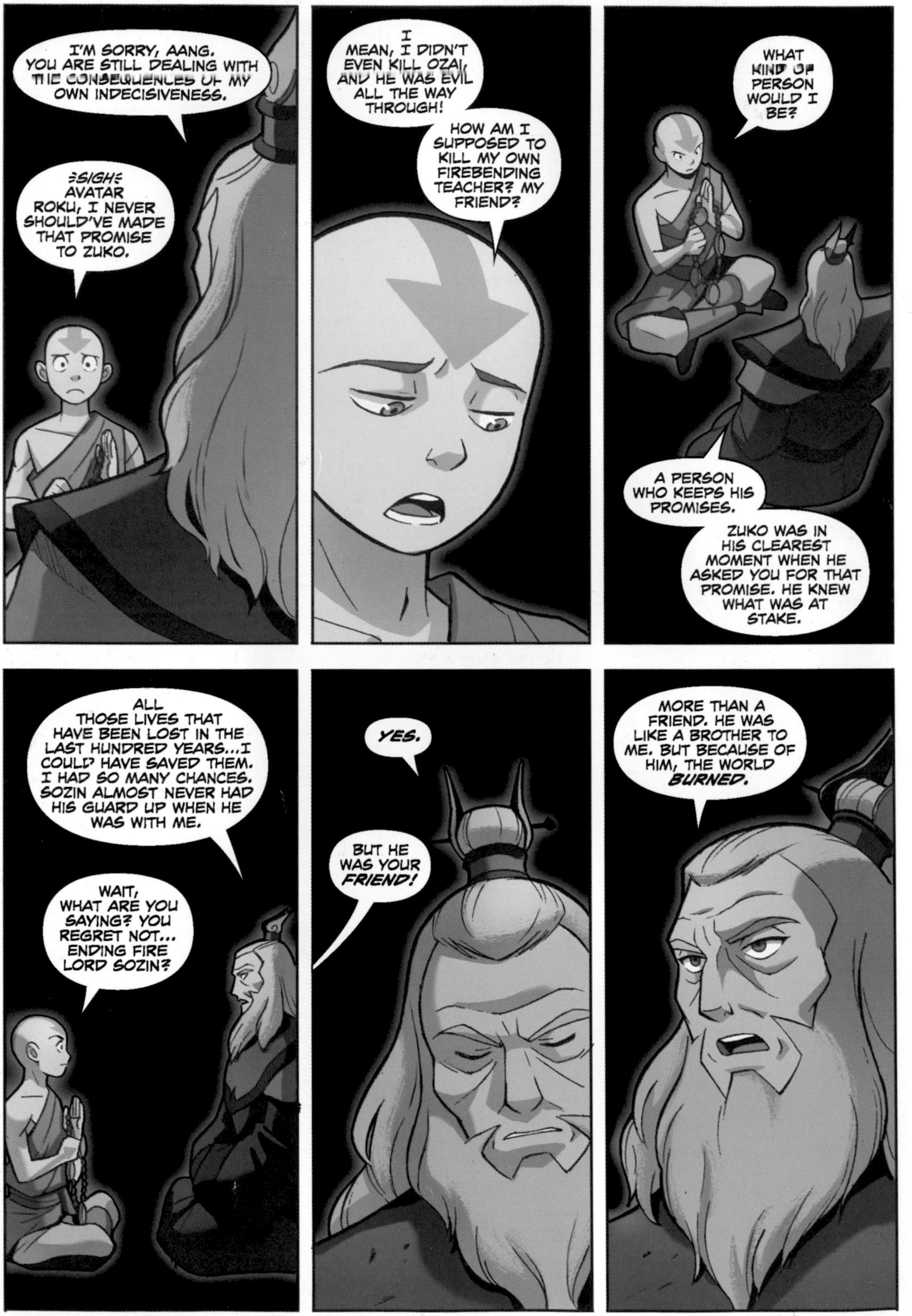
I'M SORRY, AANG. YOU ARE STILL DEALING WITH THE CONSEQUENCES OF MY OWN INDECISIVENESS.
=SIGH= AVATAR ROKU, I NEVER SHOULD'VE MADE THAT PROMISE TO ZUKO.
I MEAN, I DIDN'T EVEN KILL OZAI, AND HE WAS EVIL ALL THE WAY THROUGH!
HOW AM I SUPPOSED TO KILL MY OWN FIREBENDING TEACHER? MY FRIEND?
WHAT KIND OF PERSON WOULD I BE?
A PERSON WHO KEEPS HIS PROMISES.
ZUKO WAS IN HIS CLEAREST MOMENT WHEN HE ASKED YOU FOR THAT PROMISE. HE KNEW WHAT WAS AT STAKE.
ALL THOSE LIVES THAT HAVE BEEN LOST IN THE LAST HUNDRED YEARS...I COULD HAVE SAVED THEM. I HAD SO MANY CHANCES. SOZIN ALMOST NEVER HAD HIS GUARD UP WHEN HE WAS WITH ME.
WAIT, WHAT ARE YOU SAYING? YOU REGRET NOT... ENDING FIRE LORD SOZIN?
YES.
BUT HE WAS YOUR FRIEND!
MORE THAN A FRIEND. HE WAS LIKE A BROTHER TO ME. BUT BECAUSE OF HIM, THE WORLD BURNED.

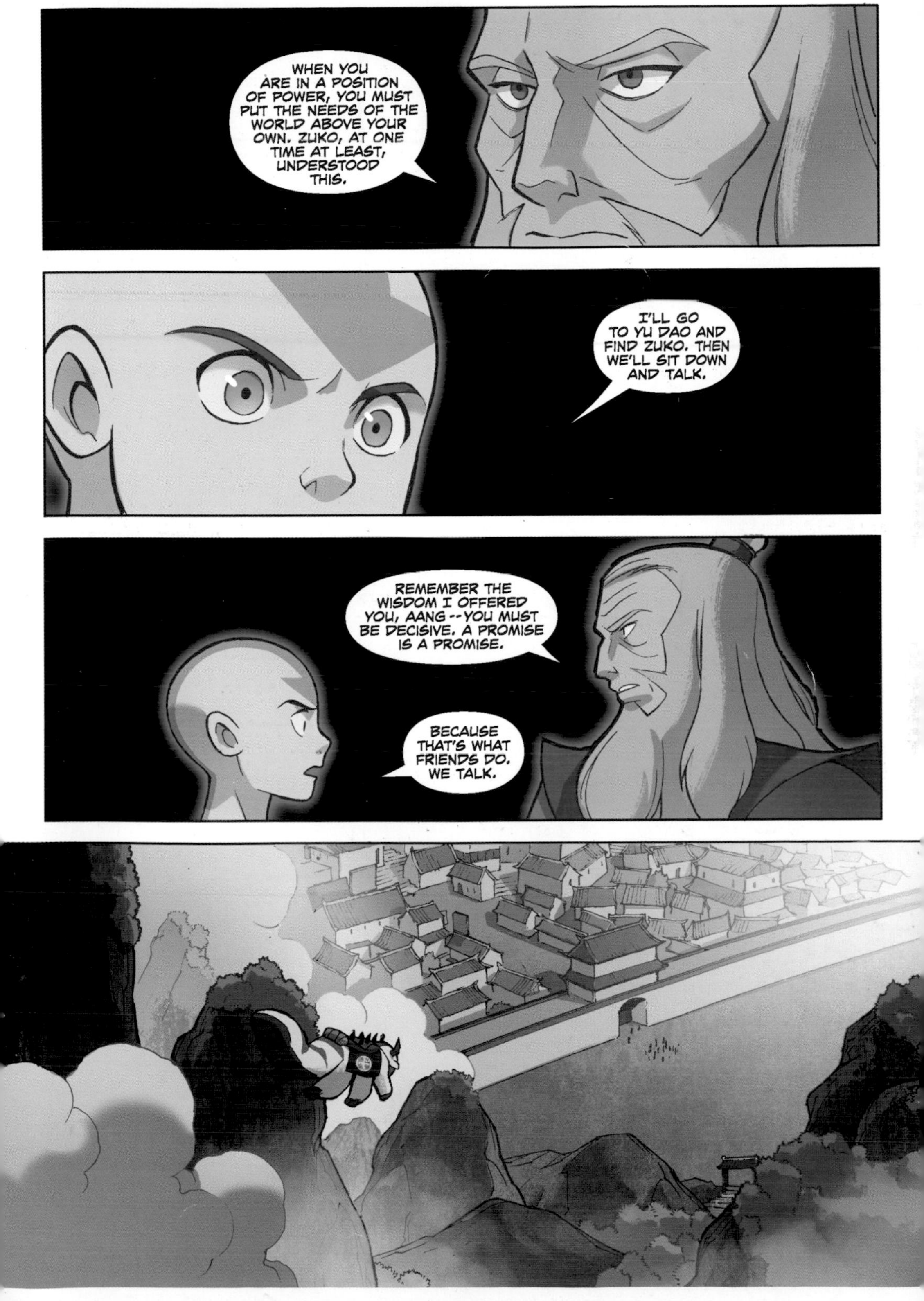
WHEN YOU ARE IN A POSITION OF POWER, YOU MUST PUT THE NEEDS OF THE WORLD ABOVE YOUR OWN. ZUKO, AT ONE TIME AT LEAST, UNDERSTOOD THIS.
I'LL GO TO YU DAO AND FIND ZUKO. THEN WE'LL SIT DOWN AND TALK.
REMEMBER THE WISDOM I OFFERED YOU, AANG--YOU MUST BE DECISIVE. A PROMISE IS A PROMISE.
BECAUSE THAT'S WHAT FRIENDS DO. WE TALK.

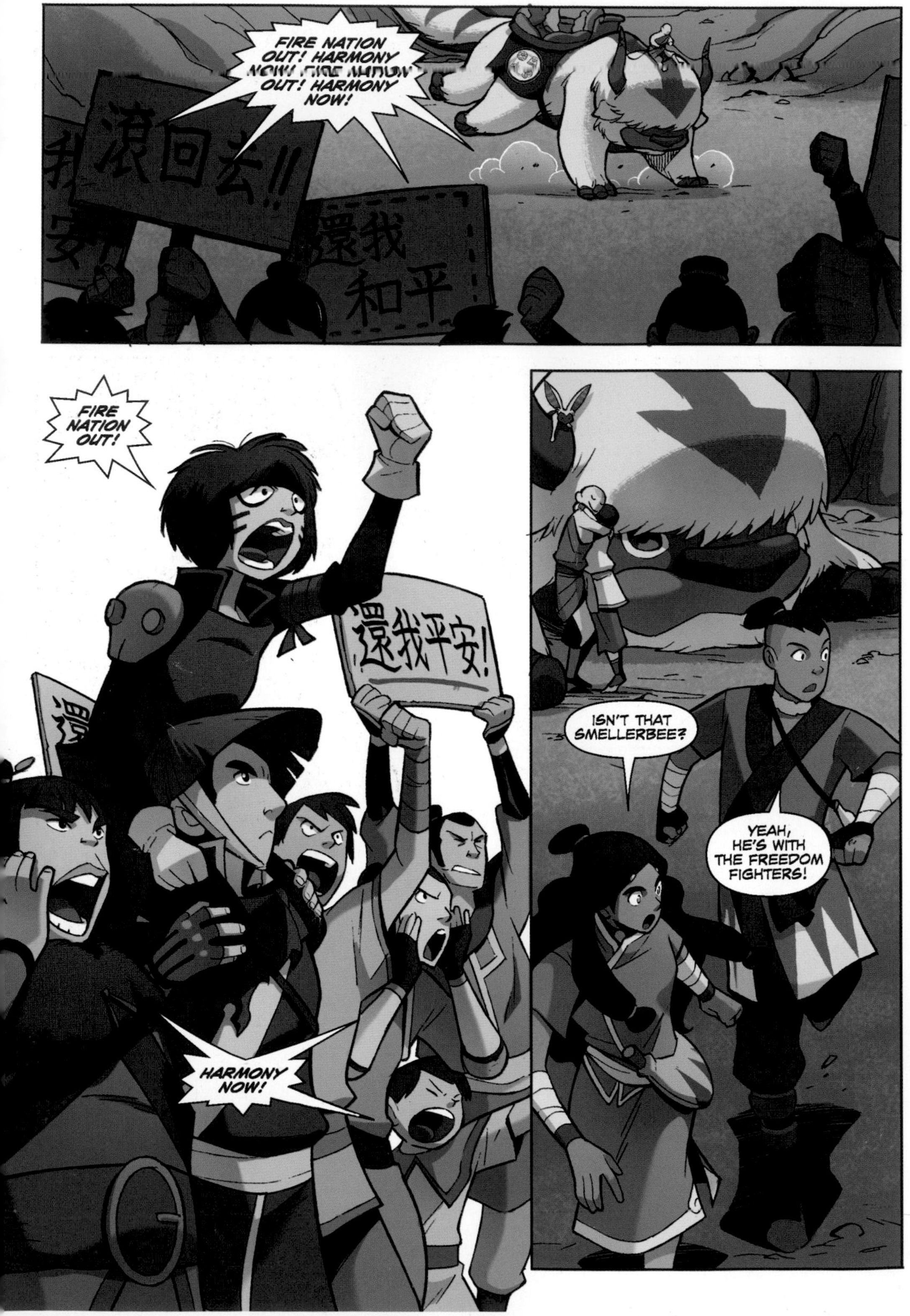
FIRE NATION OUT! HARMONY NOW! FIRE NATION OUT! HARMONY NOW!
滾回去!!
還我和平
FIRE NATION OUT!
還我平安!
HARMONY NOW!
ISN'T THAT SMELLERBEE?
YEAH, HE'S WITH THE FREEDOM FIGHTERS!

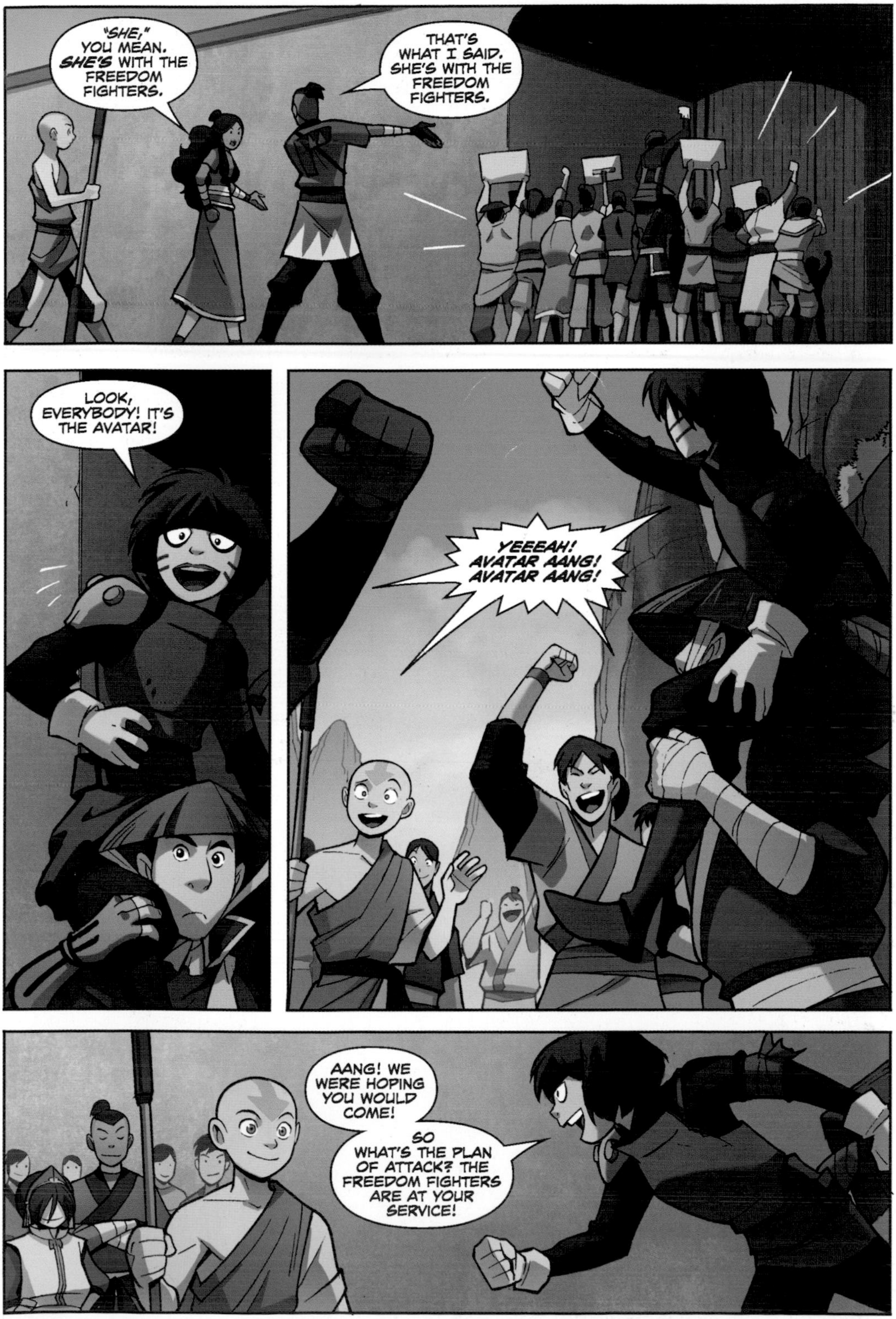
"SHE," YOU MEAN. SHE'S WITH THE FREEDOM FIGHTERS.
THAT'S WHAT I SAID. SHE'S WITH THE FREEDOM FIGHTERS.
LOOK, EVERYBODY! IT'S THE AVATAR!
YEEEAH! AVATAR AANG! AVATAR AANG!
AANG! WE WERE HOPING YOU WOULD COME!
SO WHAT'S THE PLAN OF ATTACK? THE FREEDOM FIGHTERS ARE AT YOUR SERVICE!

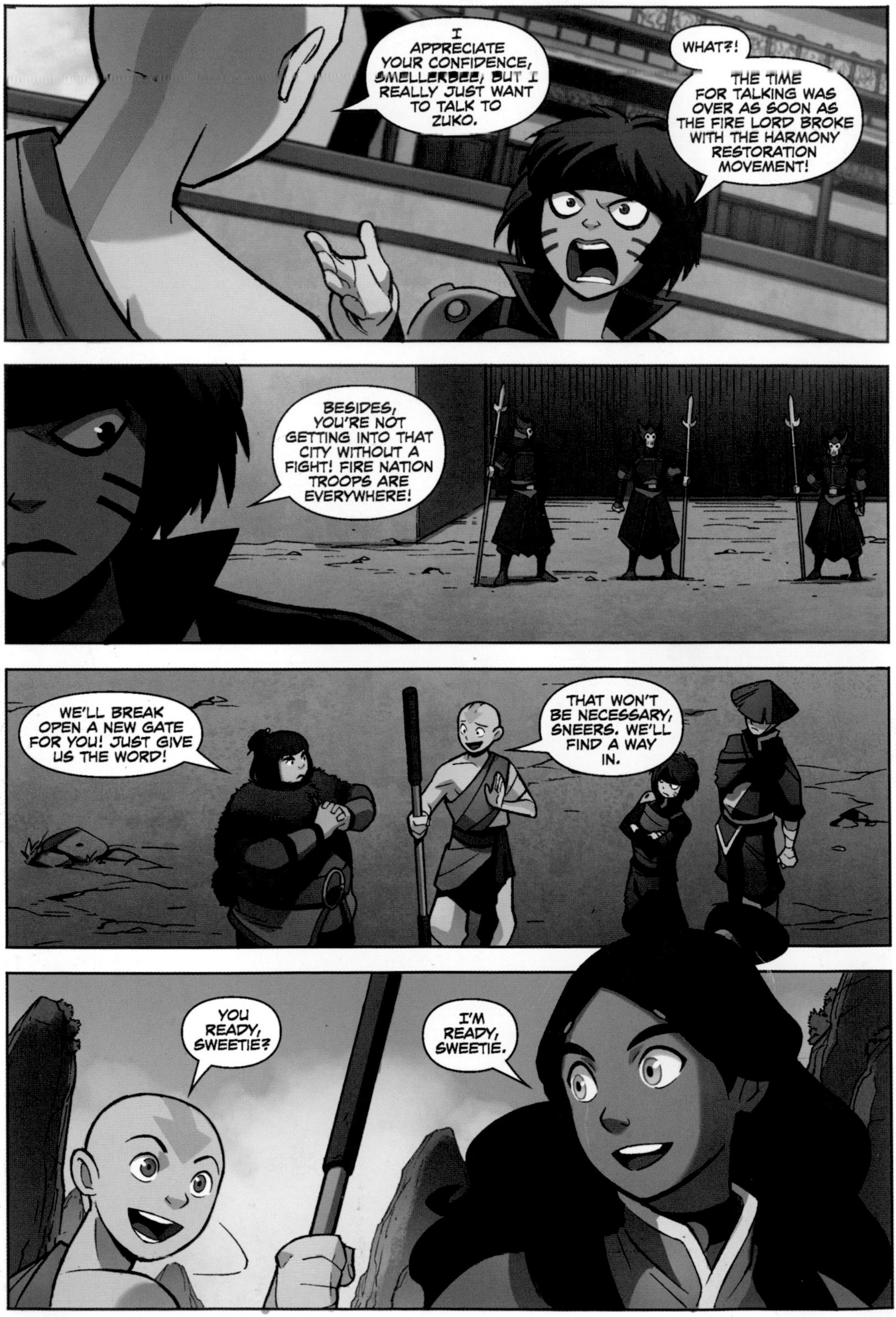
I APPRECIATE YOUR CONFIDENCE, SMELLERBEE, BUT I REALLY JUST WANT TO TALK TO ZUKO.
WHAT?!
THE TIME FOR TALKING WAS OVER AS SOON AS THE FIRE LORD BROKE WITH THE HARMONY RESTORATION MOVEMENT!
BESIDES, YOU'RE NOT GETTING INTO THAT CITY WITHOUT A FIGHT! FIRE NATION TROOPS ARE EVERYWHERE!
WE'LL BREAK OPEN A NEW GATE FOR YOU! JUST GIVE US THE WORD!
THAT WON'T BE NECESSARY, SNEERS. WE'LL FIND A WAY IN.
YOU READY, SWEETIE?
I'M READY, SWEETIE.

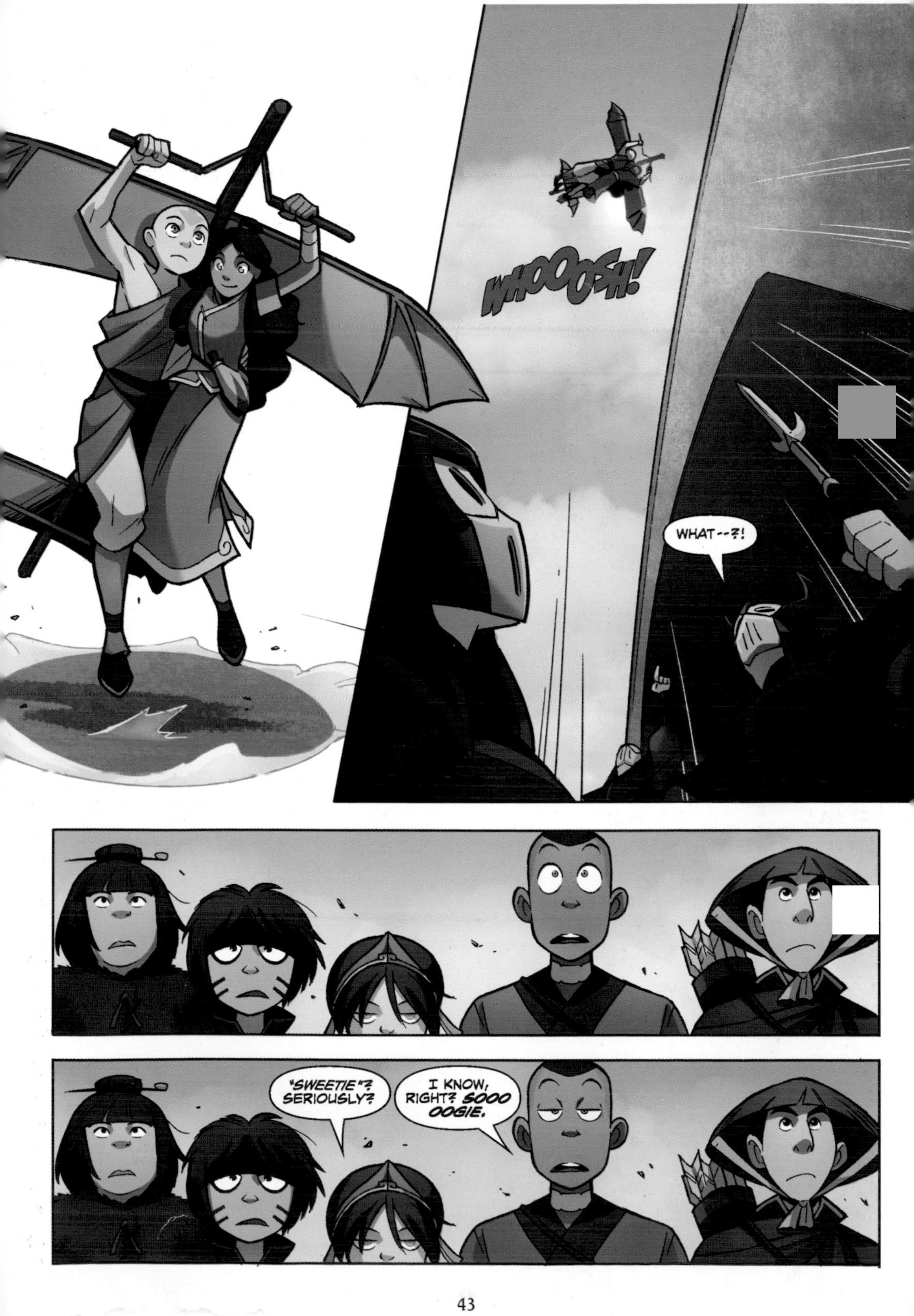
WHOOOSH!
WHAT--?!
"SWEETIE"? SERIOUSLY?
I KNOW, RIGHT? SOOO OOGIE.

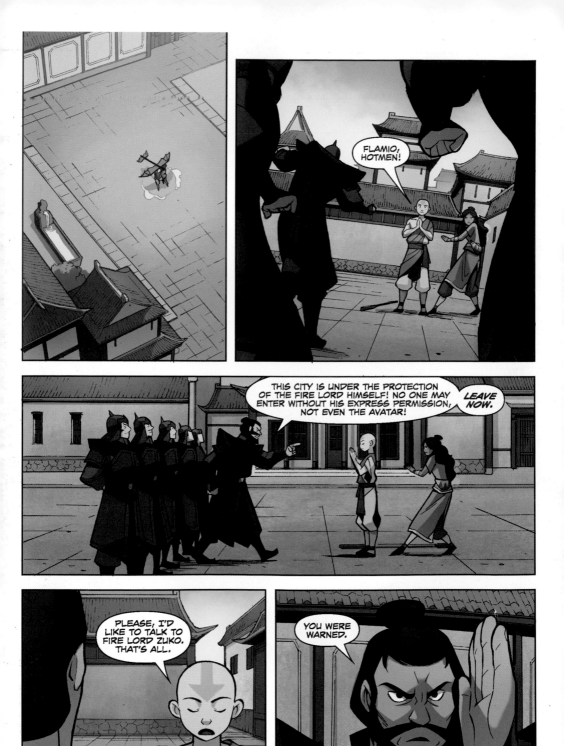

FLAMIO, HOTMEN!

THIS CITY IS UNDER THE PROTECTION OF THE FIRE LORD HIMSELF! NO ONE MAY ENTER WITHOUT HIS EXPRESS PERMISSION, NOT EVEN THE AVATAR!

LEAVE NOW.

PLEASE, I'D LIKE TO TALK TO FIRE LORD ZUKO. THAT'S ALL.

YOU WERE WARNED.

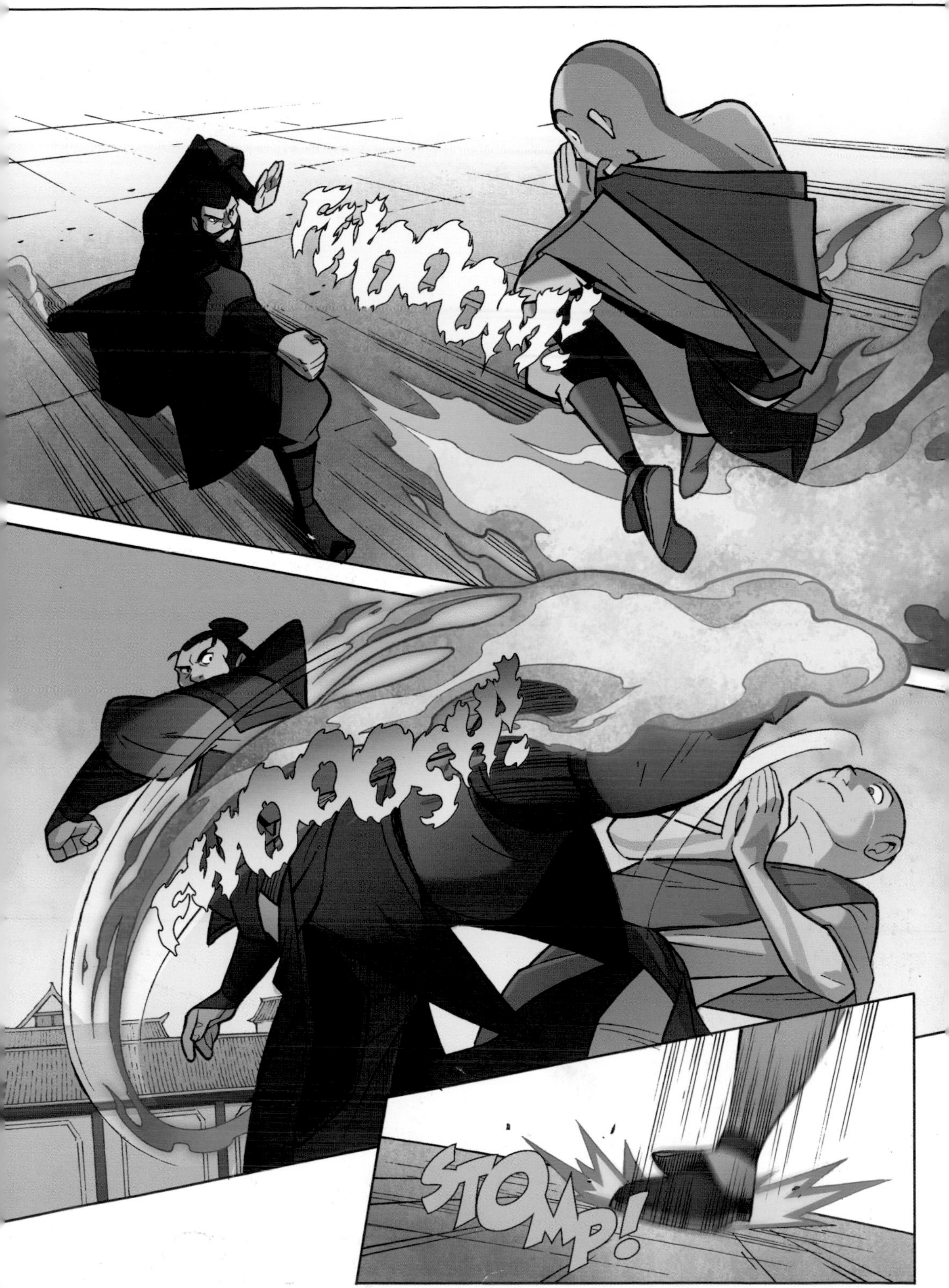
FWOOOM!
SWOOOSH!
STOMP!

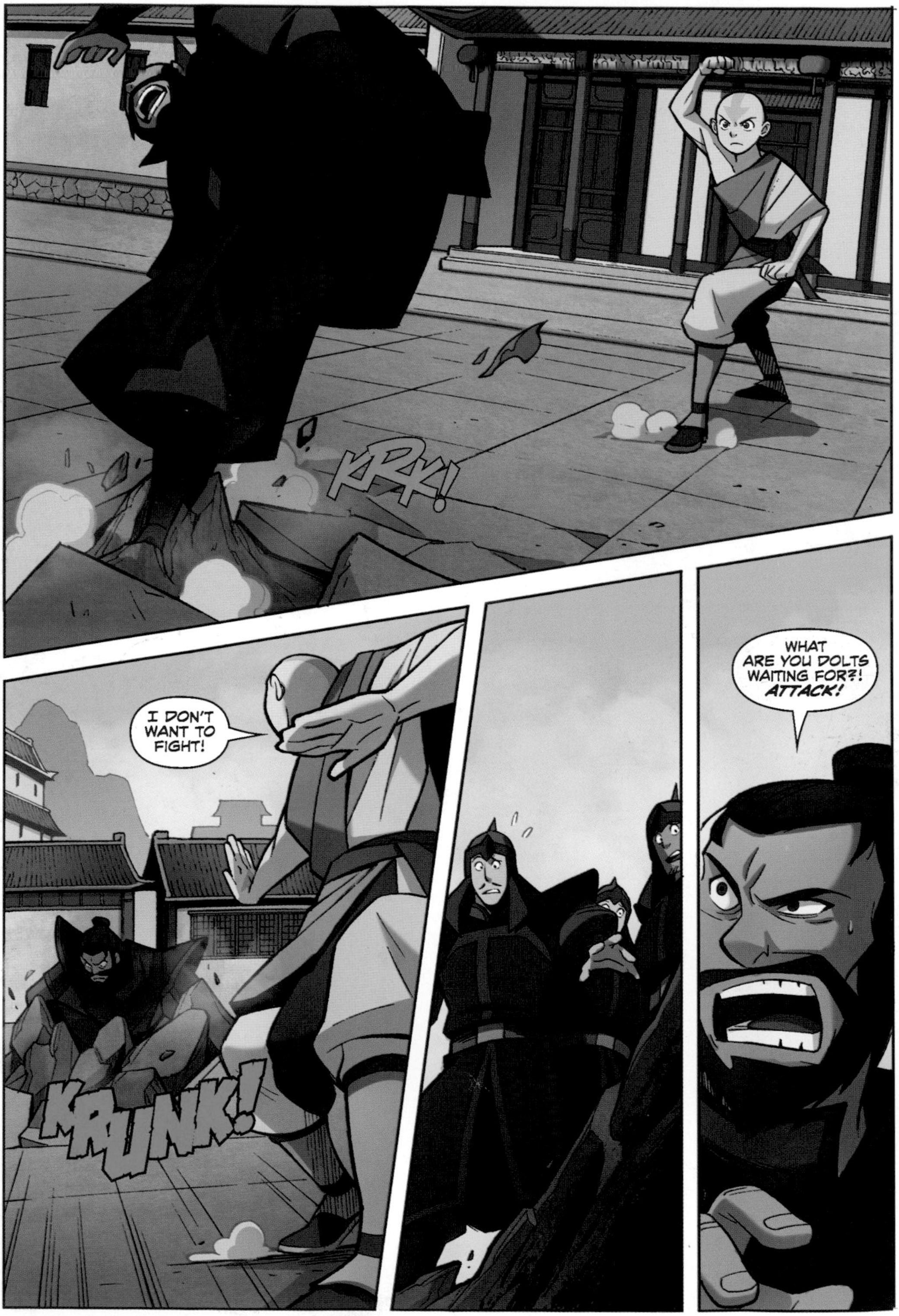
KRK!
I DON'T WANT TO FIGHT!
KRUNK!
WHAT ARE YOU DOLTS WAITING FOR?! ATTACK!

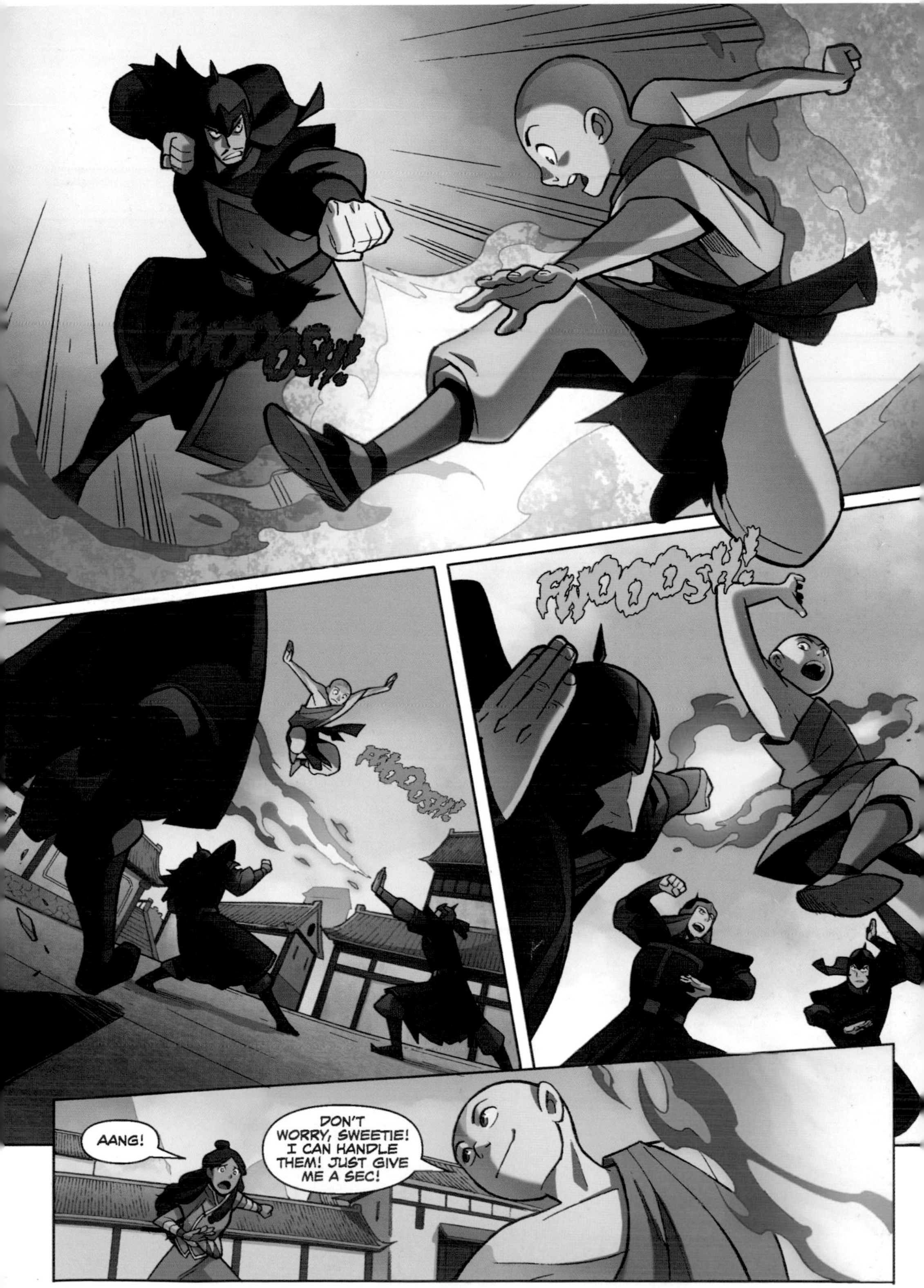
FWOOSH!
FWOOSH!
FWOOSH!
FWOOSH!
AANG!
DON'T WORRY, SWEETIE! I CAN HANDLE THEM! JUST GIVE ME A SEC!

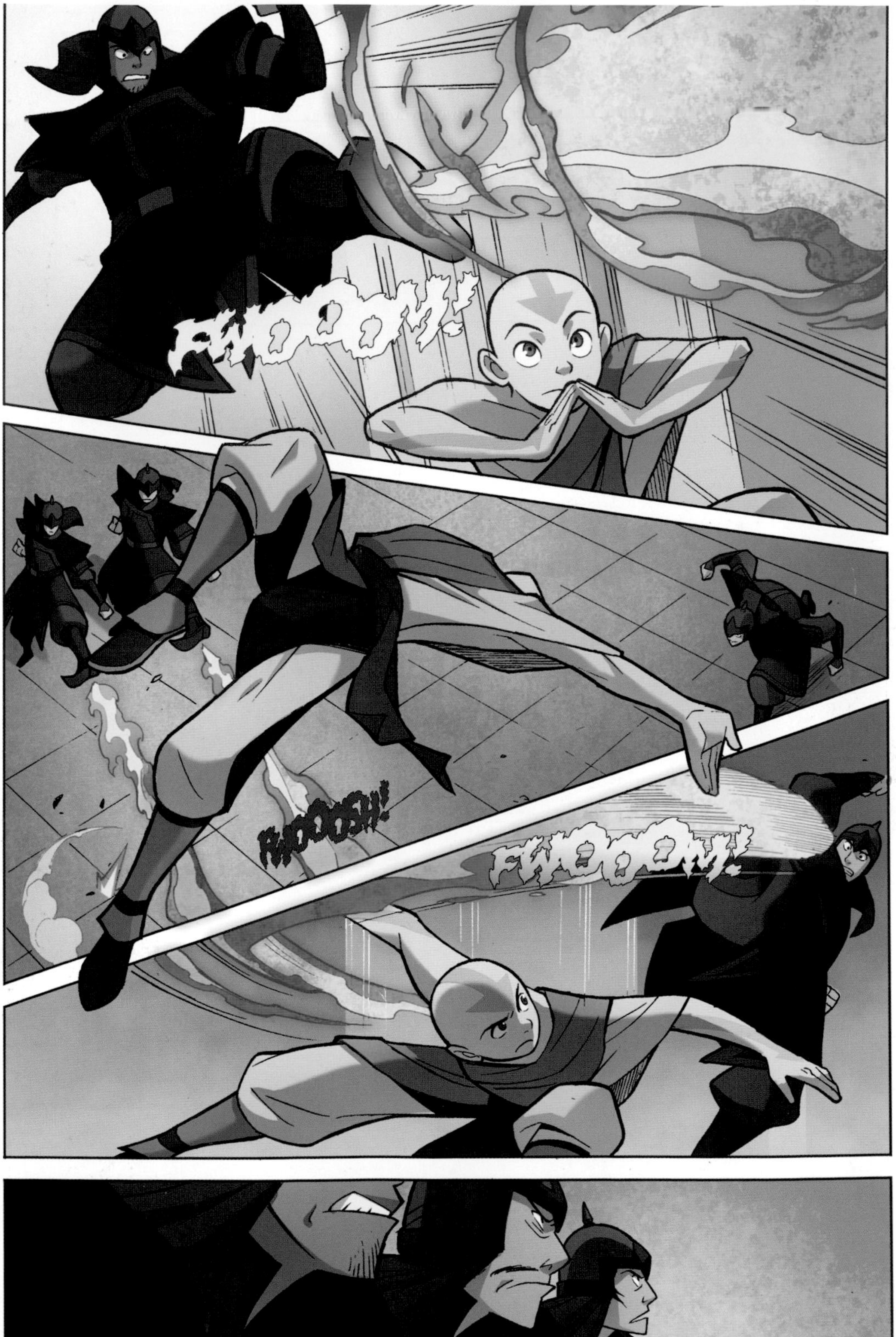
FWOOOM!
FWOOOSH!
FWOOOM!

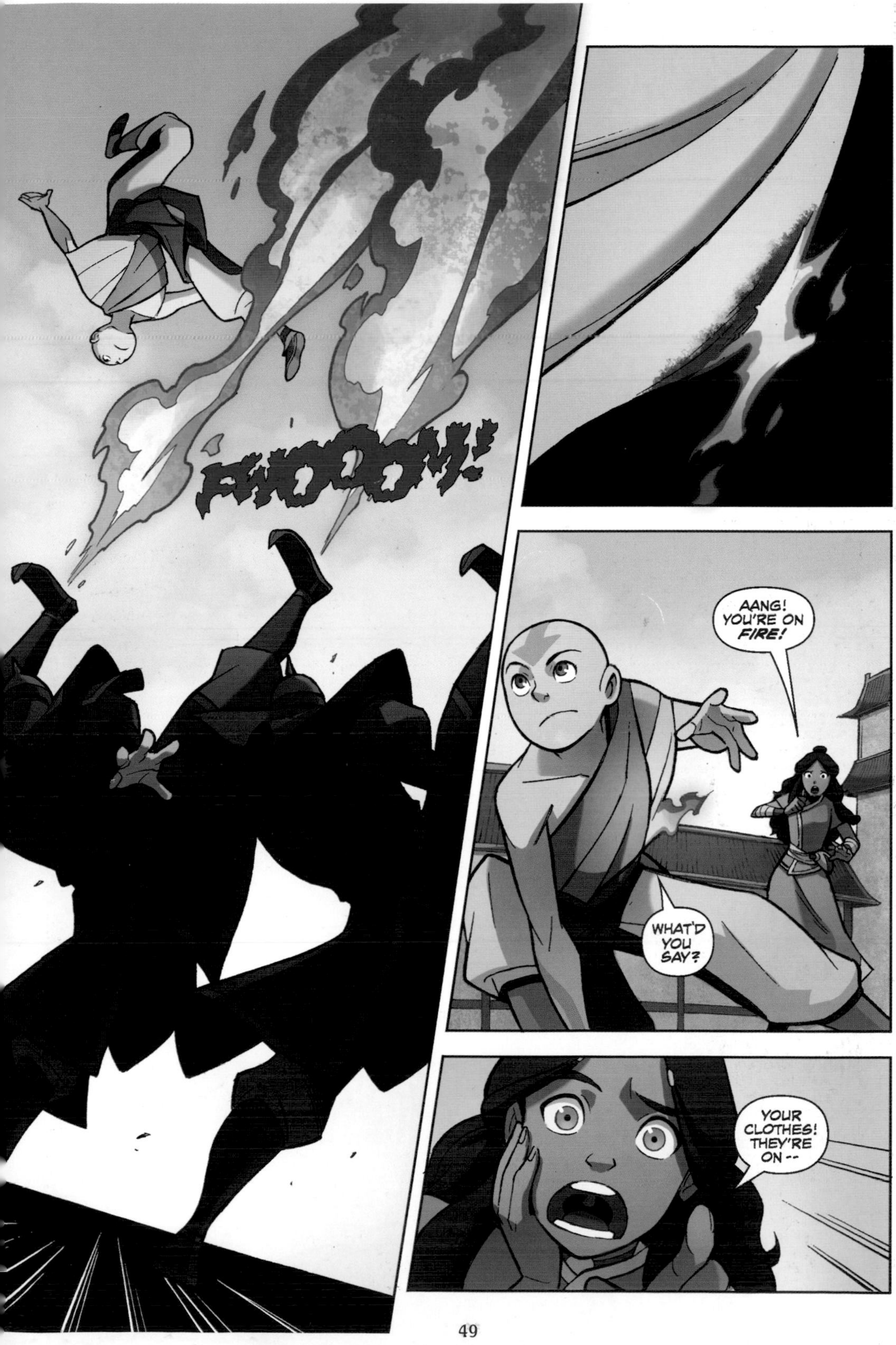
FWOOOM!
AANG! YOU'RE ON FIRE!
WHAT'D YOU SAY?
YOUR CLOTHES! THEY'RE ON --

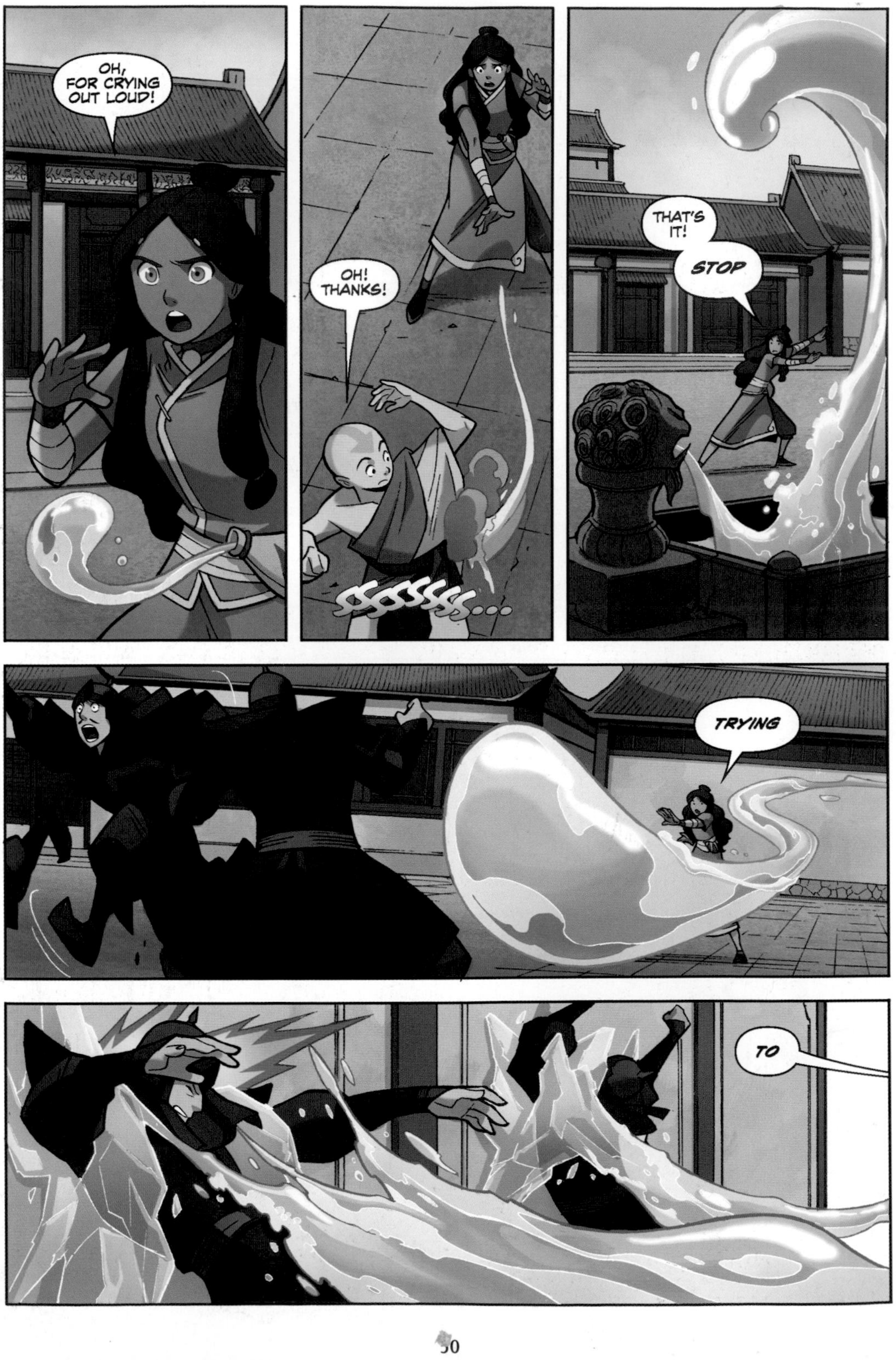
OH, FOR CRYING OUT LOUD!
OH! THANKS!
SSSSSSS...
THAT'S IT!
STOP
TRYING
TO

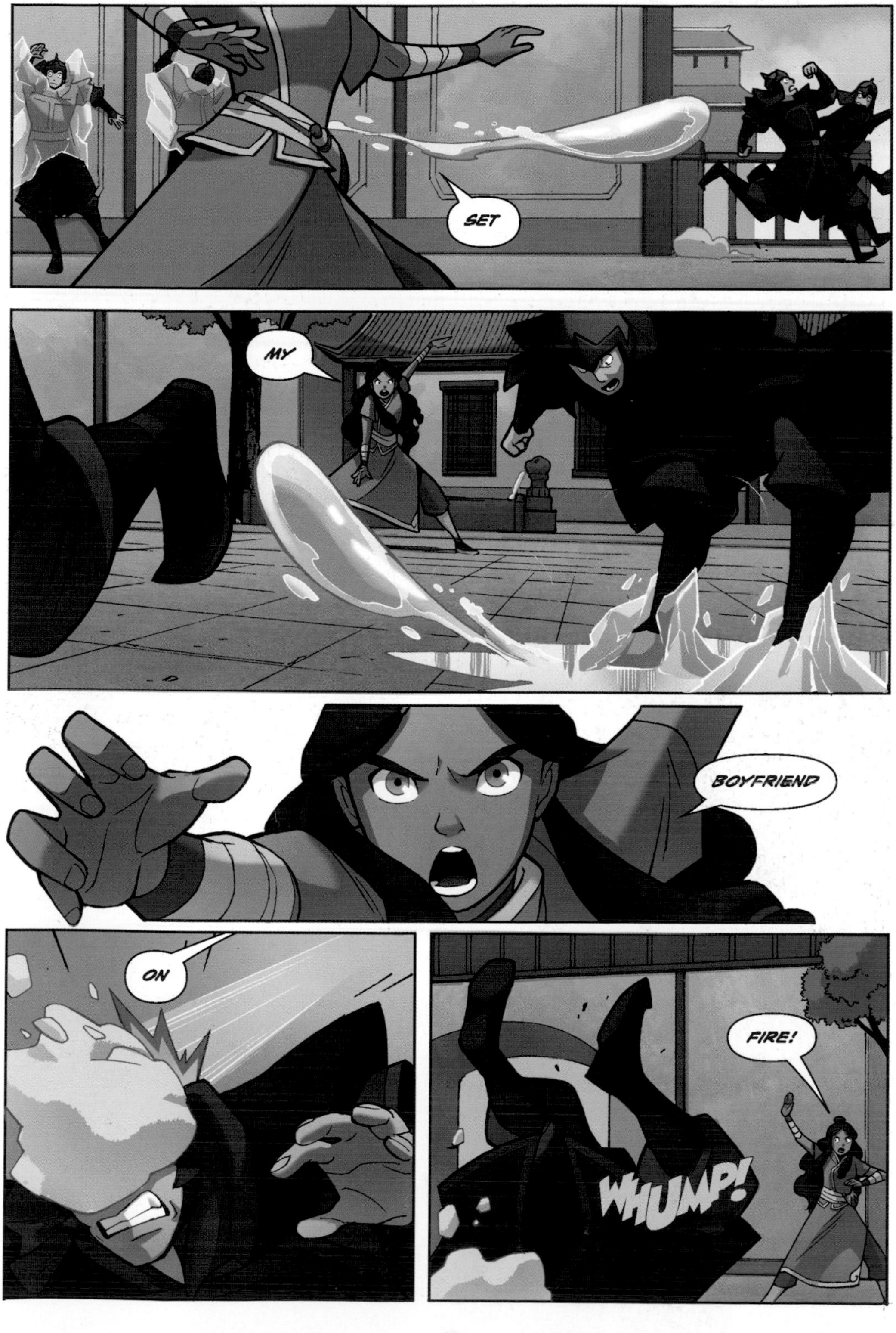
SET
MY
BOYFRIEND
ON
FIRE!
WHUMP!

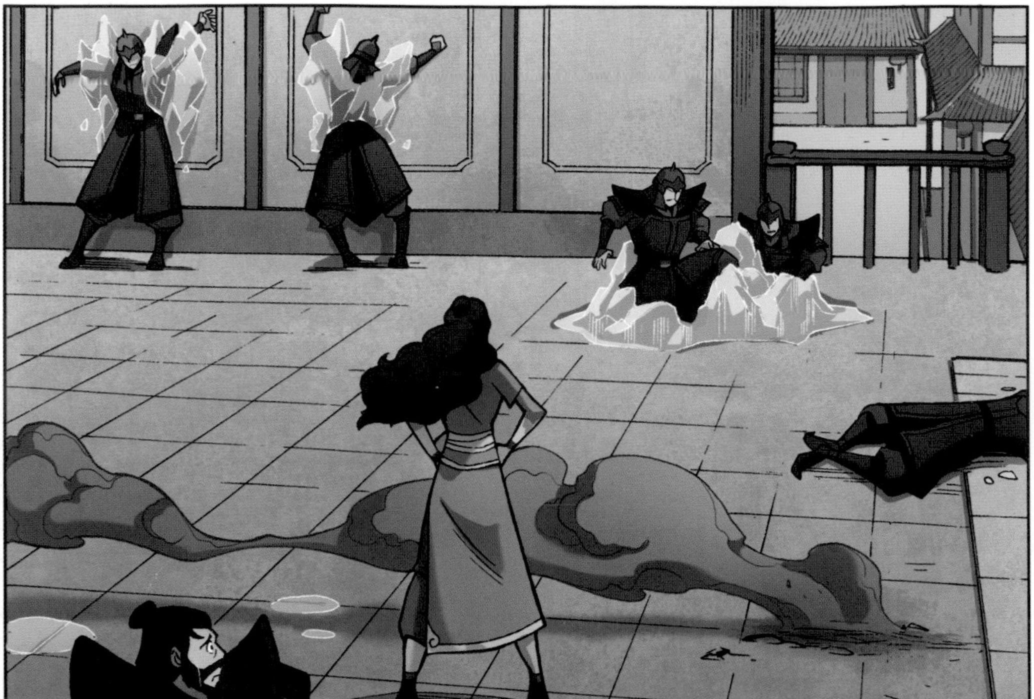

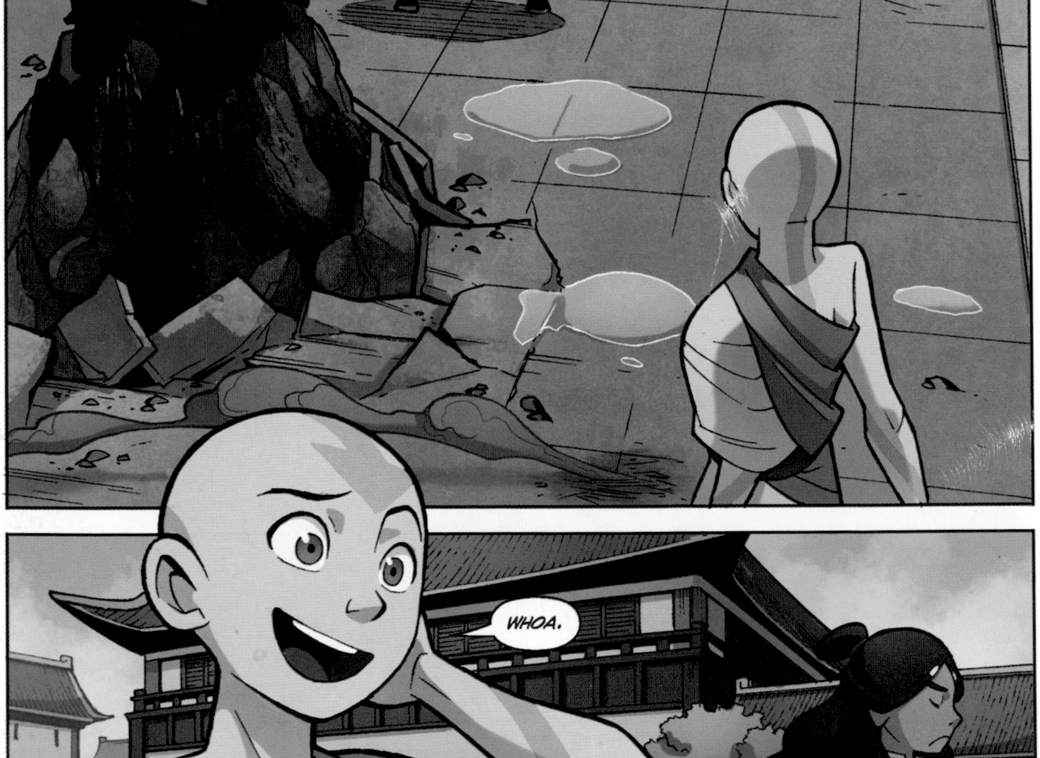
WHOA.

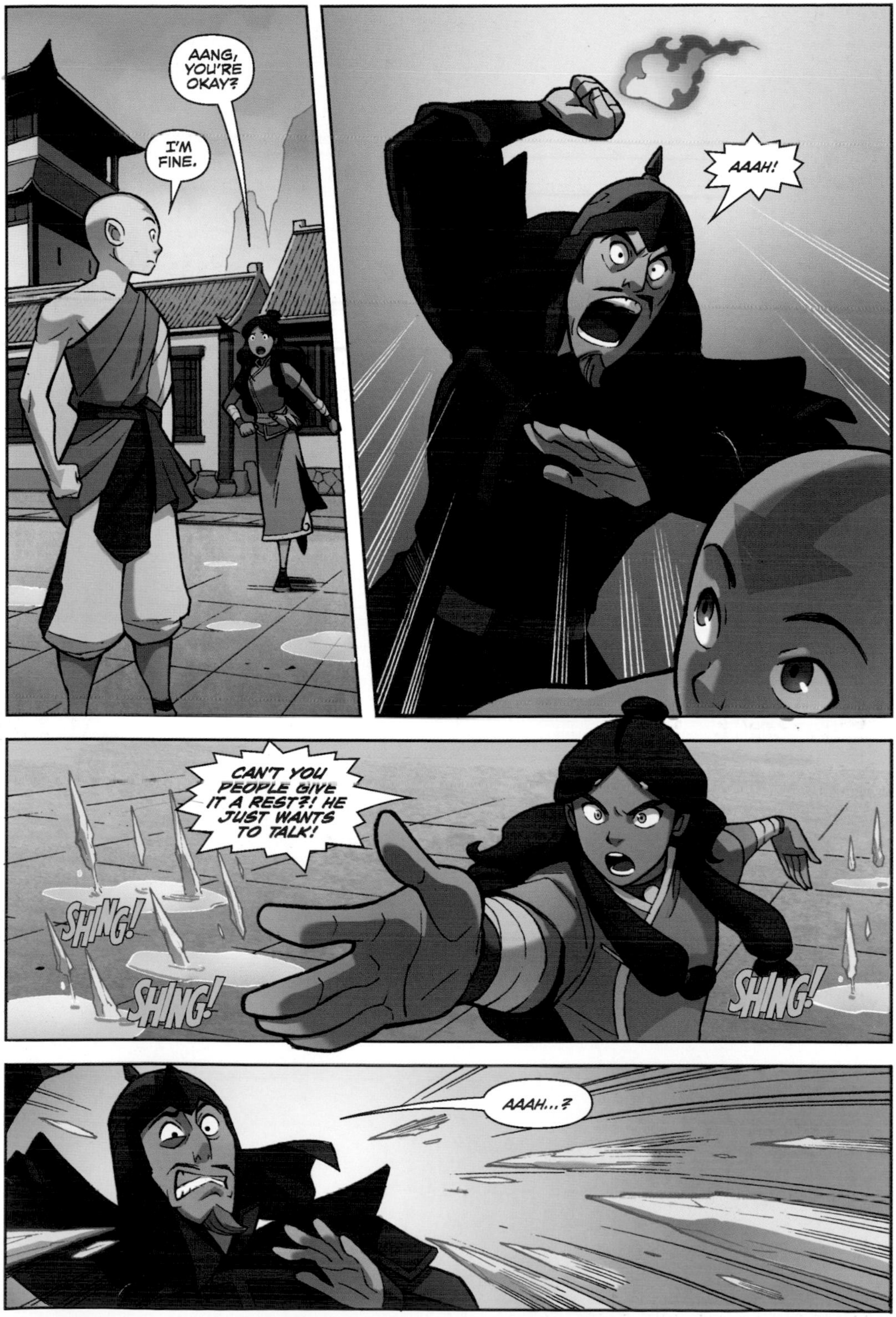
AANG, YOU'RE OKAY?
I'M FINE.
AAAH!
CAN'T YOU PEOPLE GIVE IT A REST?! HE JUST WANTS TO TALK!
SHING!
SHING!
SHING!
AAAH...?

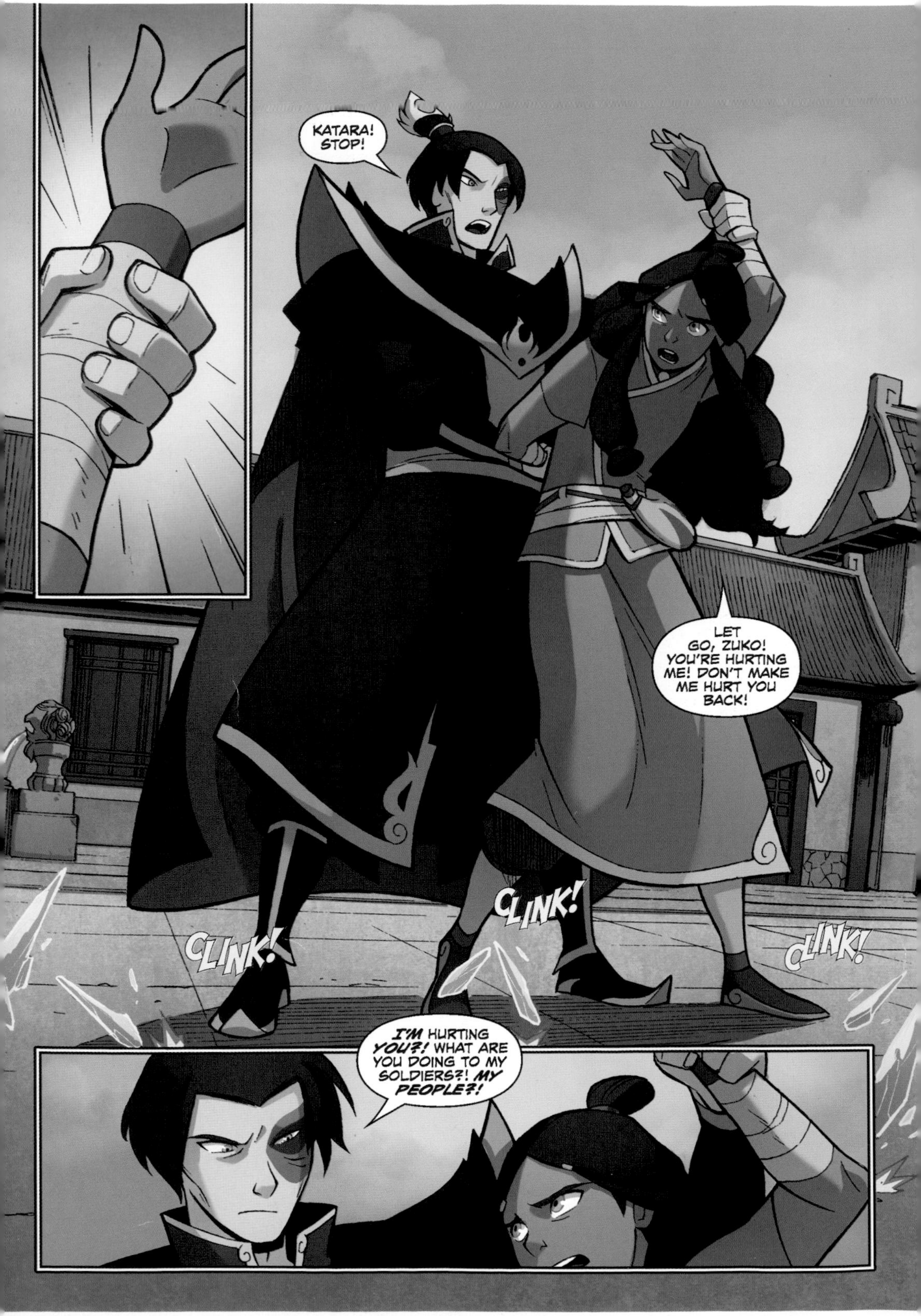
KATARA! STOP!
LET GO, ZUKO! YOU'RE HURTING ME! DON'T MAKE ME HURT YOU BACK!
CLINK!
CLINK!
CLINK!
I'M HURTING YOU?! WHAT ARE YOU DOING TO MY SOLDIERS?! MY PEOPLE?!

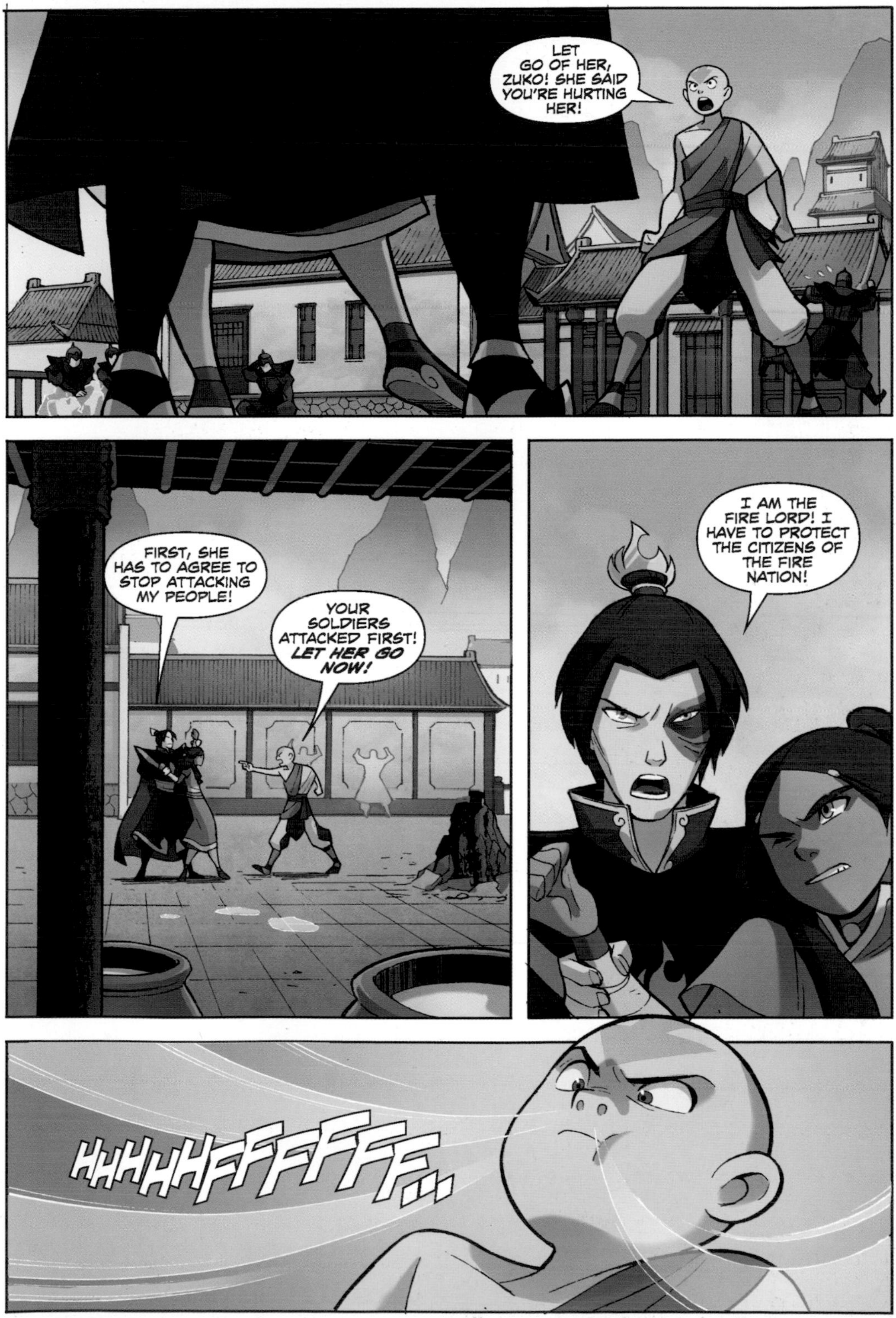
LET GO OF HER, ZUKO! SHE SAID YOU'RE HURTING HER!
FIRST, SHE HAS TO AGREE TO STOP ATTACKING MY PEOPLE!
YOUR SOLDIERS ATTACKED FIRST! LET HER GO NOW!
I AM THE FIRE LORD! I HAVE TO PROTECT THE CITIZENS OF THE FIRE NATION!
HHHHHFFFFFFF...

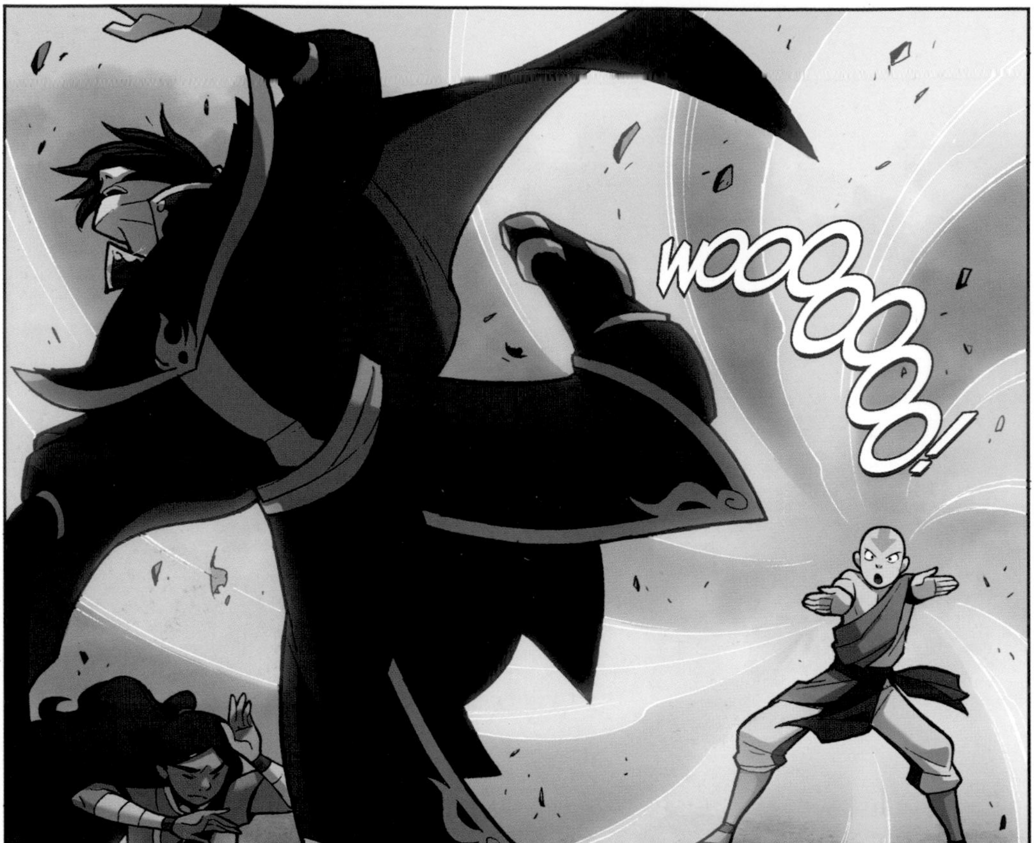
WOOOOOOOO!

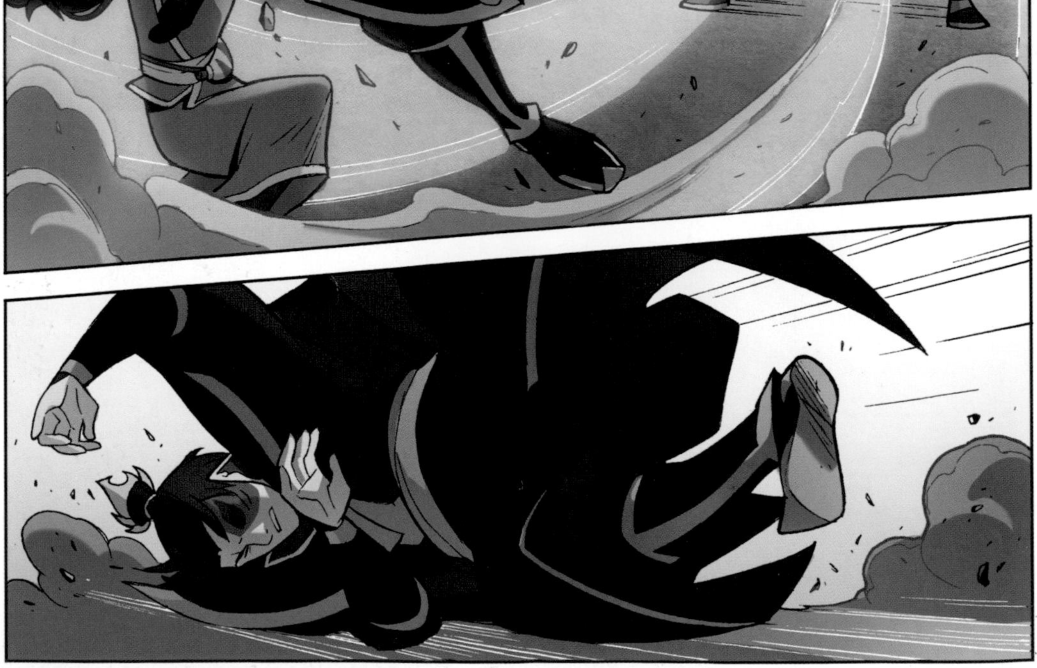

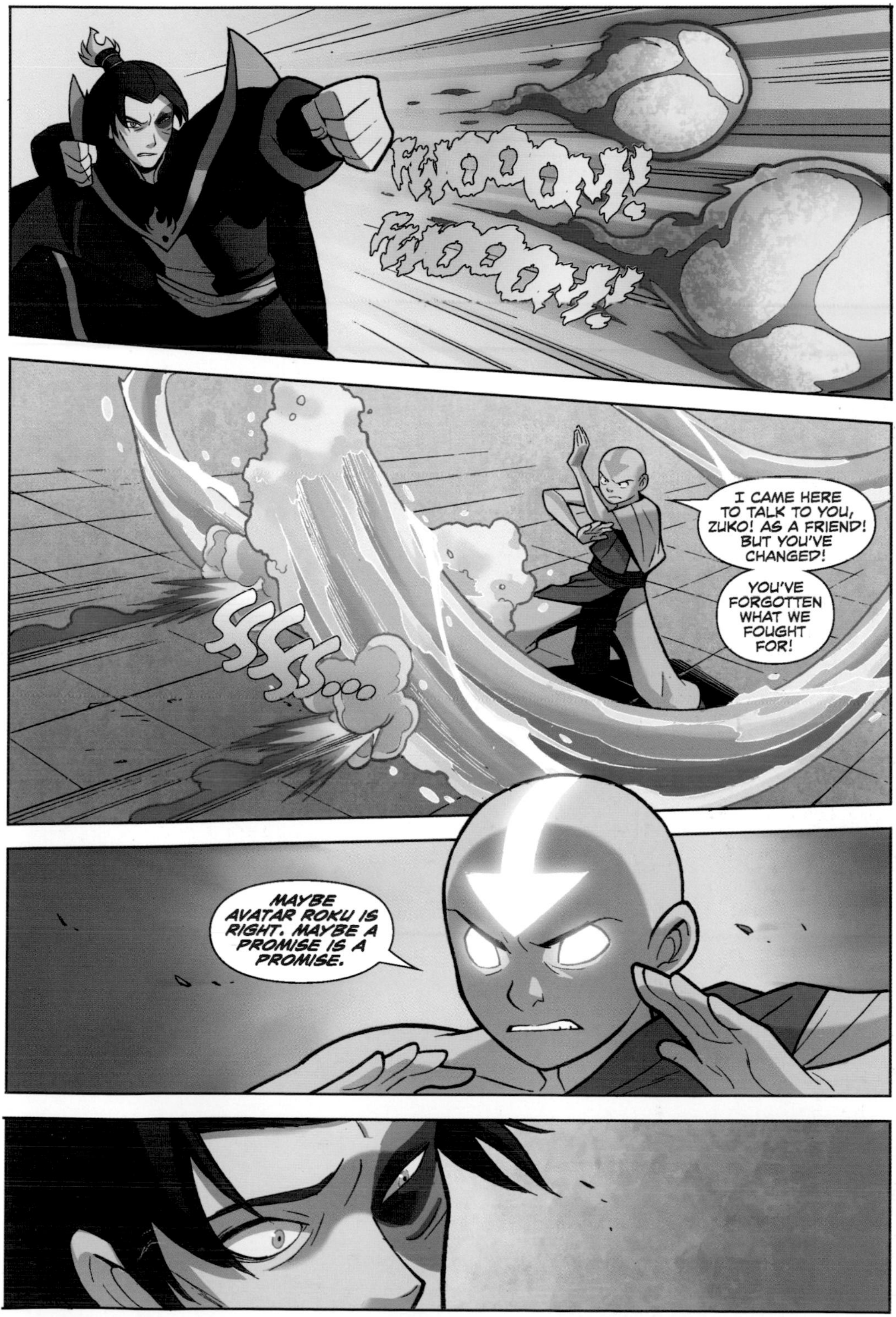
FWOOOM!
FWOOOM!
I CAME HERE TO TALK TO YOU, ZUKO! AS A FRIEND! BUT YOU'VE CHANGED!
YOU'VE FORGOTTEN WHAT WE FOUGHT FOR!
SSSS...
MAYBE AVATAR ROKU IS RIGHT. MAYBE A PROMISE IS A PROMISE.

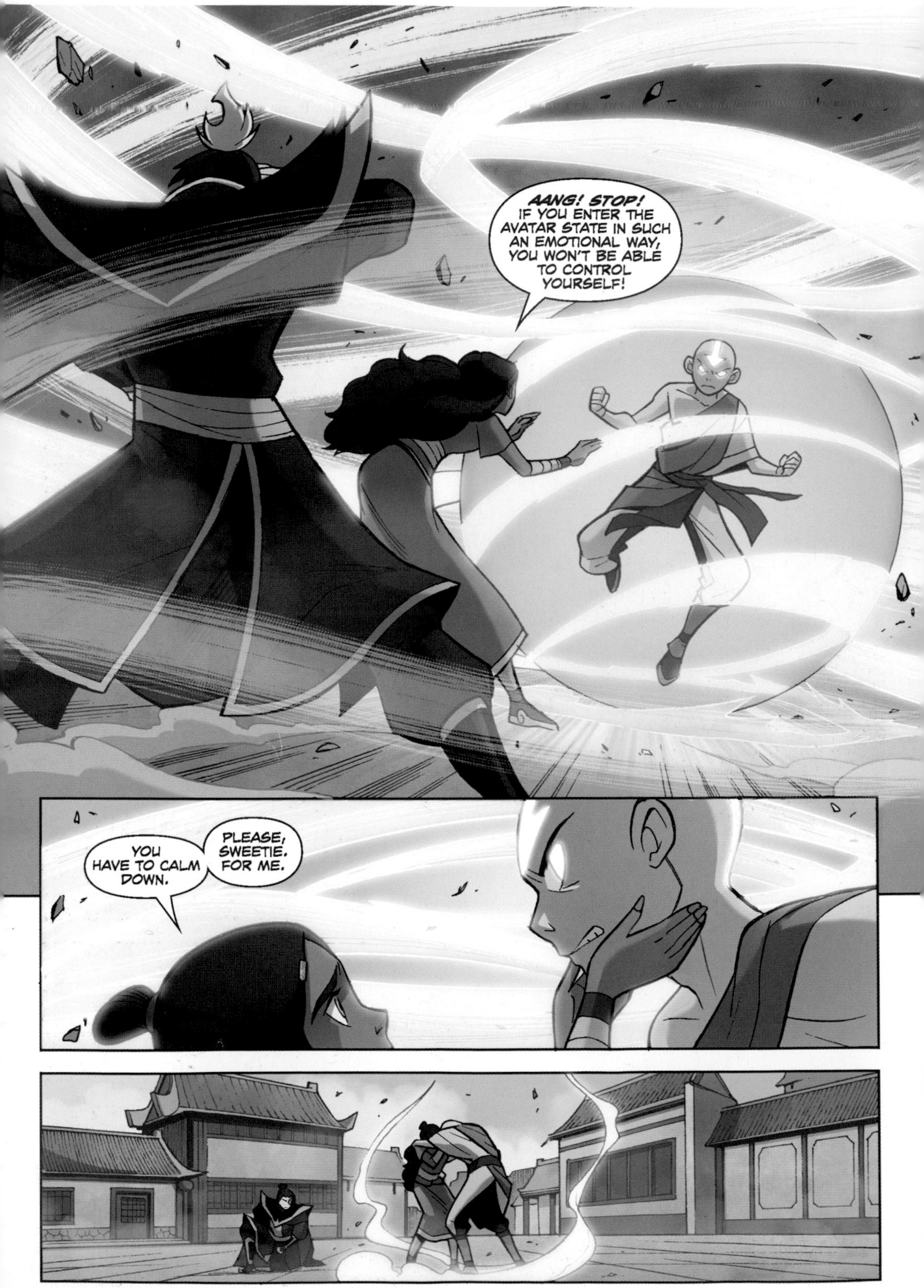
AANG! STOP! IF YOU ENTER THE AVATAR STATE IN SUCH AN EMOTIONAL WAY, YOU WON'T BE ABLE TO CONTROL YOURSELF!
YOU HAVE TO CALM DOWN.
PLEASE, SWEETIE. FOR ME.

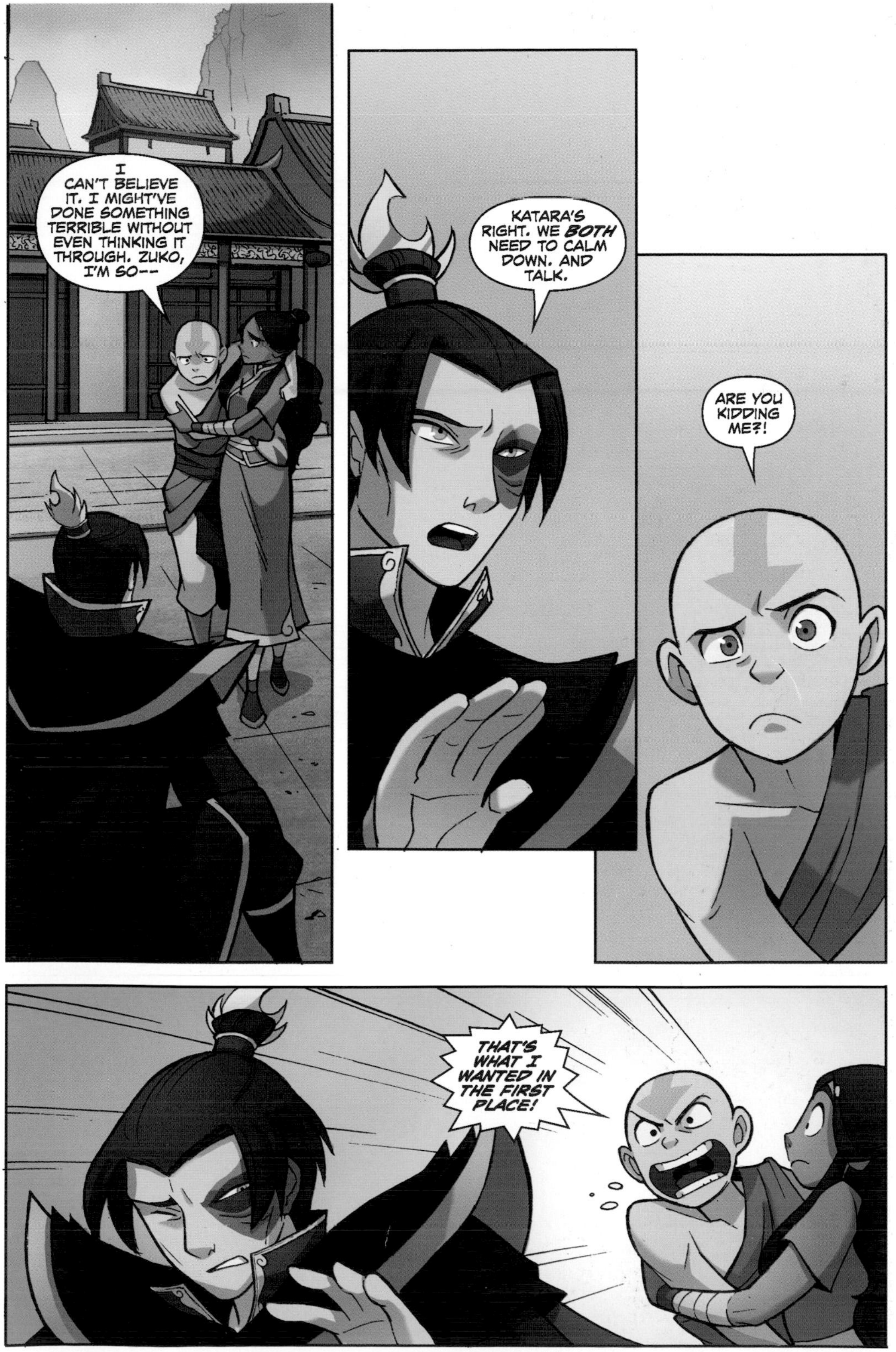
I CAN'T BELIEVE IT. I MIGHT'VE DONE SOMETHING TERRIBLE WITHOUT EVEN THINKING IT THROUGH. ZUKO, I'M SO--
KATARA'S RIGHT. WE *BOTH* NEED TO CALM DOWN. AND TALK.
ARE YOU KIDDING ME?!
THAT'S WHAT I WANTED IN THE FIRST PLACE!

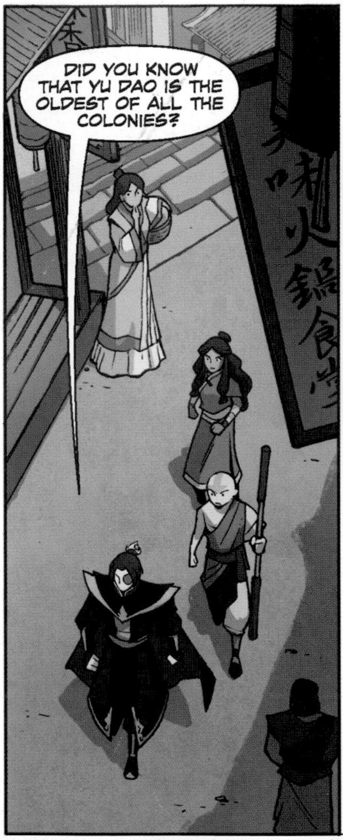
DID YOU KNOW THAT YU DAO IS THE OLDEST OF ALL THE COLONIES?

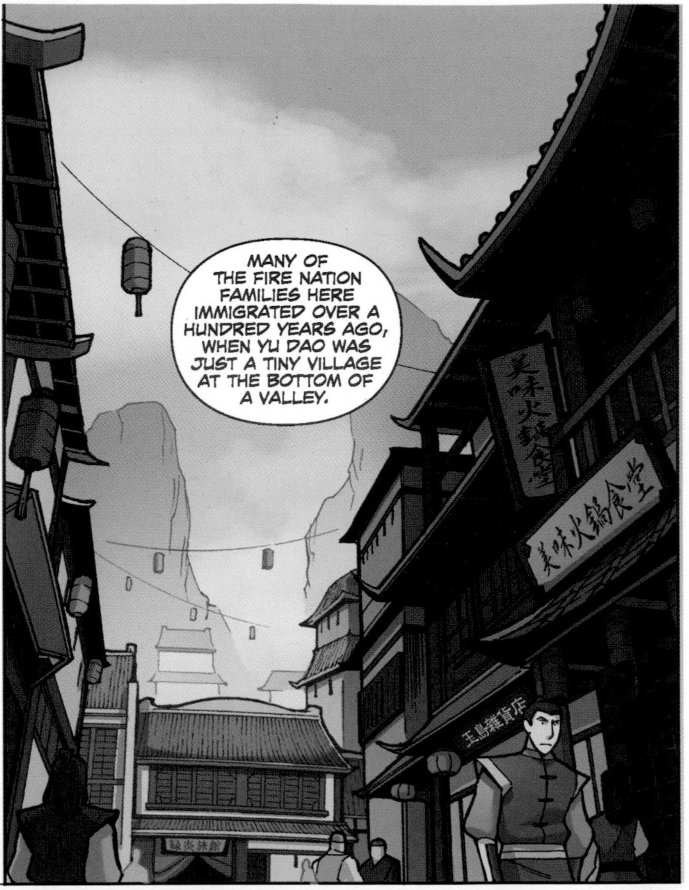
MANY OF THE FIRE NATION FAMILIES HERE IMMIGRATED OVER A HUNDRED YEARS AGO, WHEN YU DAO WAS JUST A TINY VILLAGE AT THE BOTTOM OF A VALLEY.
美味火鍋食堂
美味火鍋食堂

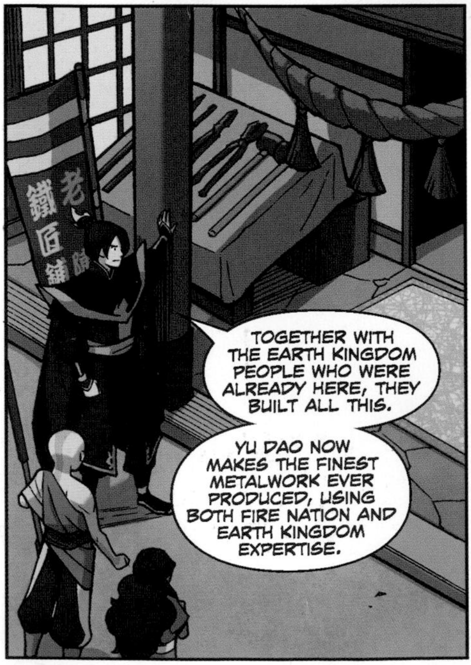
TOGETHER WITH THE EARTH KINGDOM PEOPLE WHO WERE ALREADY HERE, THEY BUILT ALL THIS.
YU DAO NOW MAKES THE FINEST METALWORK EVER PRODUCED, USING BOTH FIRE NATION AND EARTH KINGDOM EXPERTISE.

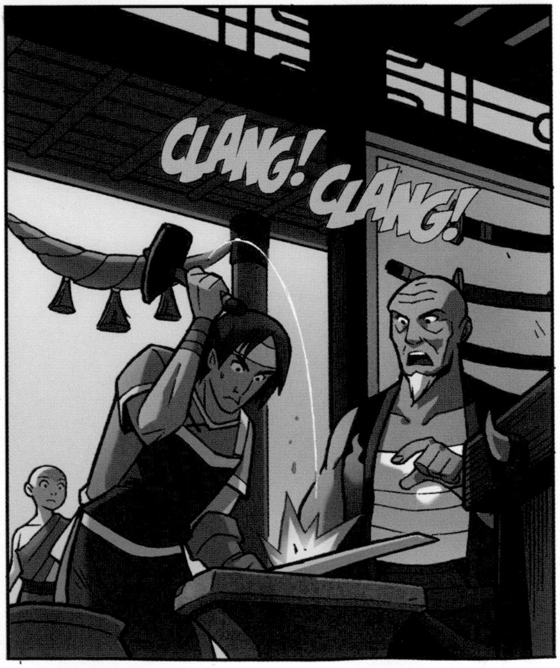
CLANG! CLANG!

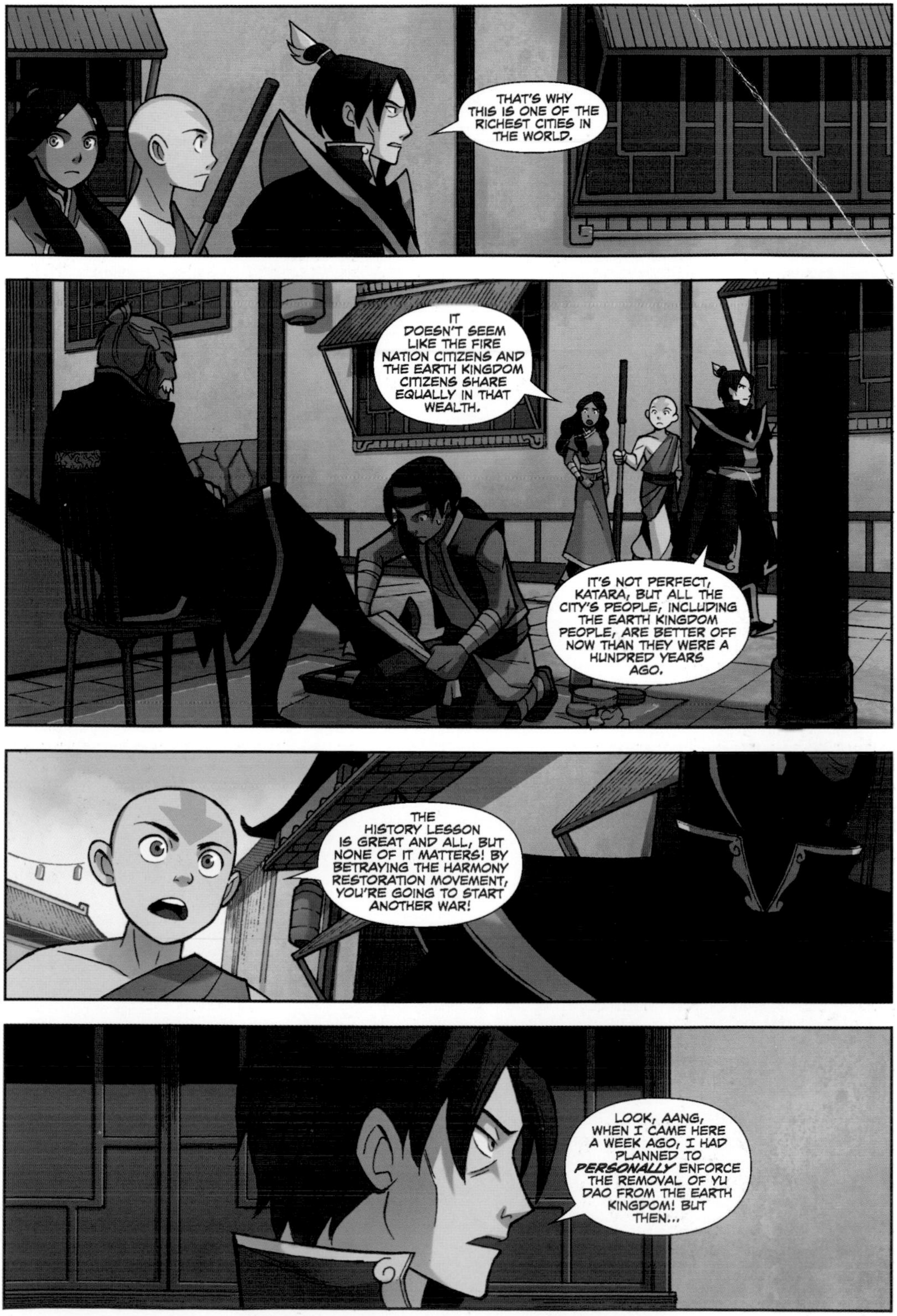
THAT'S WHY THIS IS ONE OF THE RICHEST CITIES IN THE WORLD.
IT DOESN'T SEEM LIKE THE FIRE NATION CITIZENS AND THE EARTH KINGDOM CITIZENS SHARE EQUALLY IN THAT WEALTH.
IT'S NOT PERFECT, KATARA, BUT ALL THE CITY'S PEOPLE, INCLUDING THE EARTH KINGDOM PEOPLE, ARE BETTER OFF NOW THAN THEY WERE A HUNDRED YEARS AGO.
THE HISTORY LESSON IS GREAT AND ALL, BUT NONE OF IT MATTERS! BY BETRAYING THE HARMONY RESTORATION MOVEMENT, YOU'RE GOING TO START ANOTHER WAR!
LOOK, AANG, WHEN I CAME HERE A WEEK AGO, I HAD PLANNED TO *PERSONALLY* ENFORCE THE REMOVAL OF YU DAO FROM THE EARTH KINGDOM! BUT THEN...

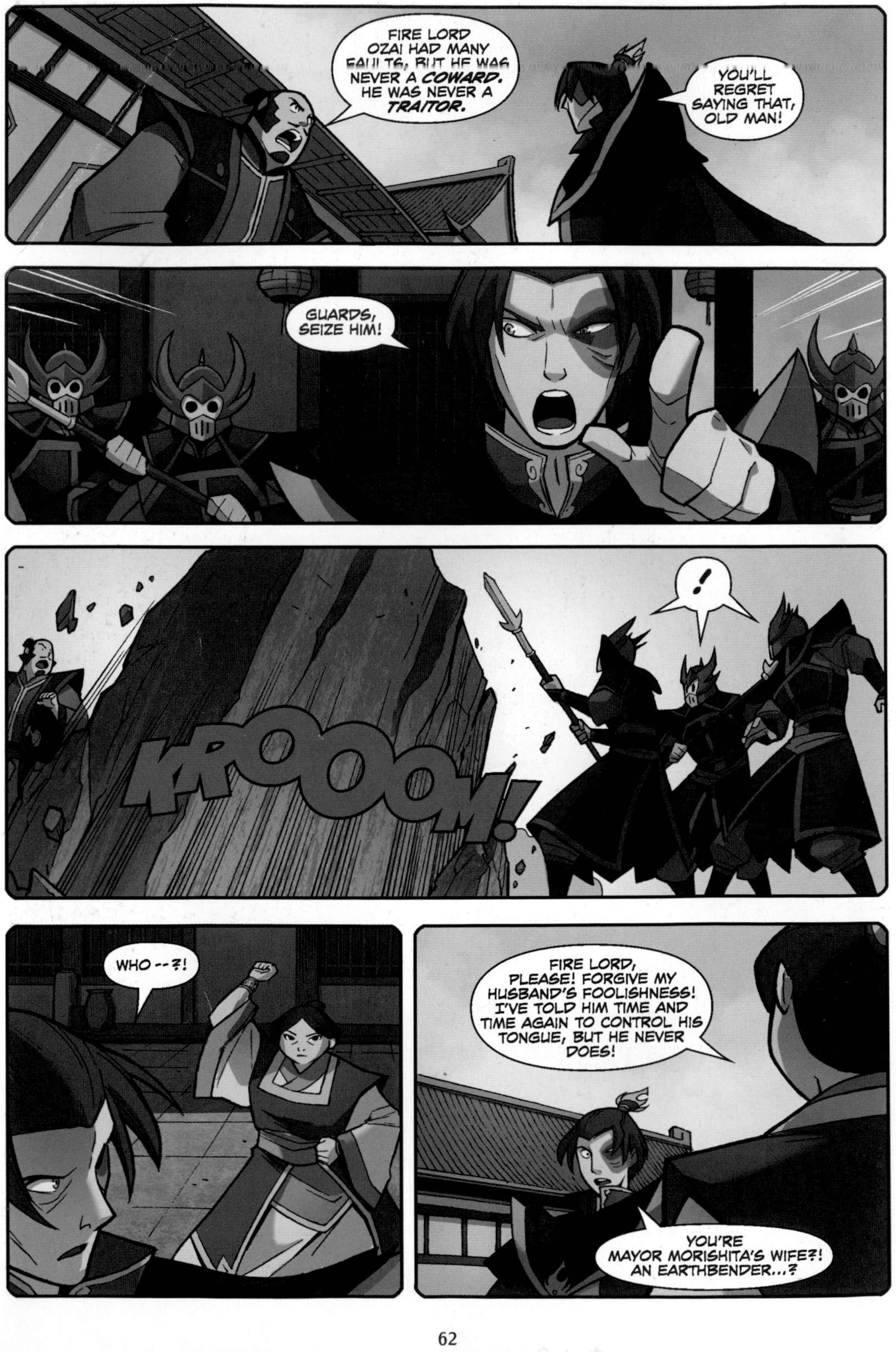
FIRE LORD OZAI HAD MANY FAULTS, BUT HE WAS NEVER A COWARD. HE WAS NEVER A TRAITOR.
YOU'LL REGRET SAYING THAT, OLD MAN!
GUARDS, SEIZE HIM!
KROOOOM!
!
WHO --?!
FIRE LORD, PLEASE! FORGIVE MY HUSBAND'S FOOLISHNESS! I'VE TOLD HIM TIME AND TIME AGAIN TO CONTROL HIS TONGUE, BUT HE NEVER DOES!
YOU'RE MAYOR MORISHITA'S WIFE?! AN EARTHBENDER...?

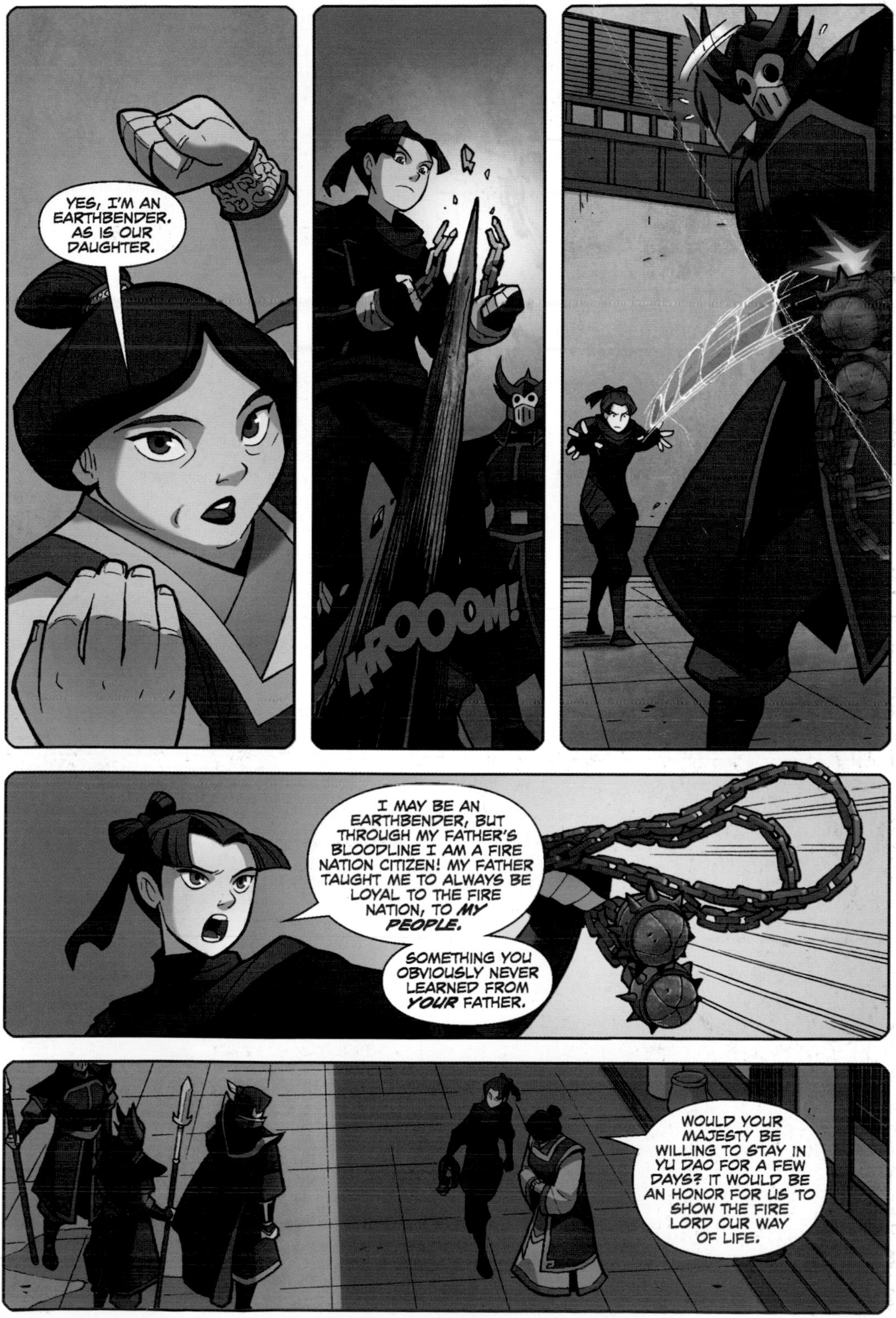
YES, I'M AN EARTHBENDER. AS IS OUR DAUGHTER.
KROOOOM!
I MAY BE AN EARTHBENDER, BUT THROUGH MY FATHER'S BLOODLINE I AM A FIRE NATION CITIZEN! MY FATHER TAUGHT ME TO ALWAYS BE LOYAL TO THE FIRE NATION, TO *MY PEOPLE.*
SOMETHING YOU OBVIOUSLY NEVER LEARNED FROM *YOUR* FATHER.
WOULD YOUR MAJESTY BE WILLING TO STAY IN YU DAO FOR A FEW DAYS? IT WOULD BE AN HONOR FOR US TO SHOW THE FIRE LORD OUR WAY OF LIFE.

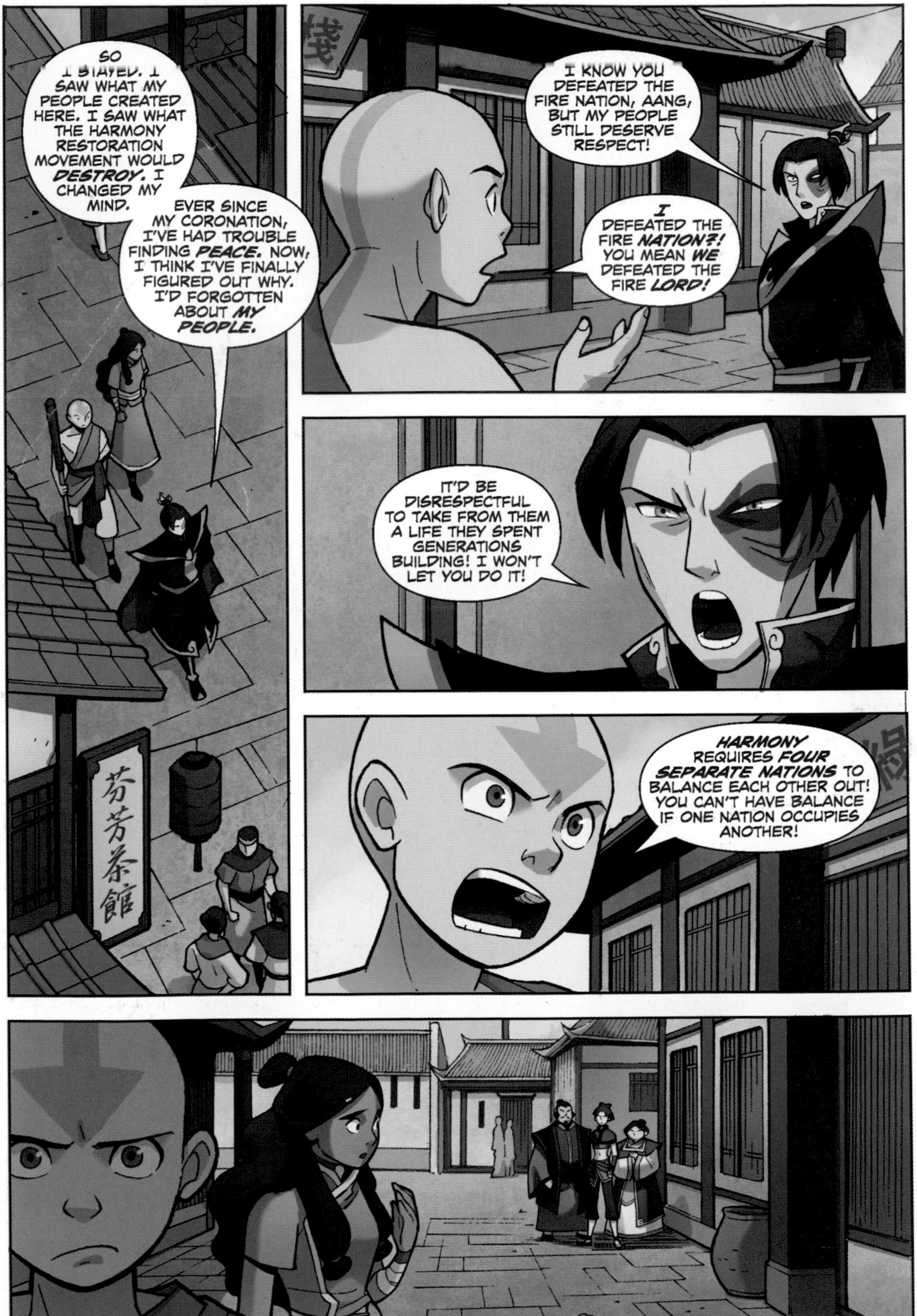
SO I STAYED. I SAW WHAT MY PEOPLE CREATED HERE. I SAW WHAT THE HARMONY RESTORATION MOVEMENT WOULD DESTROY. I CHANGED MY MIND.
EVER SINCE MY CORONATION, I'VE HAD TROUBLE FINDING PEACE. NOW, I THINK I'VE FINALLY FIGURED OUT WHY. I'D FORGOTTEN ABOUT MY PEOPLE.
芳芳茶館
I KNOW YOU DEFEATED THE FIRE NATION, AANG, BUT MY PEOPLE STILL DESERVE RESPECT!
I DEFEATED THE FIRE NATION?! YOU MEAN WE DEFEATED THE FIRE LORD!
IT'D BE DISRESPECTFUL TO TAKE FROM THEM A LIFE THEY SPENT GENERATIONS BUILDING! I WON'T LET YOU DO IT!
HARMONY REQUIRES FOUR SEPARATE NATIONS TO BALANCE EACH OTHER OUT! YOU CAN'T HAVE BALANCE IF ONE NATION OCCUPIES ANOTHER!

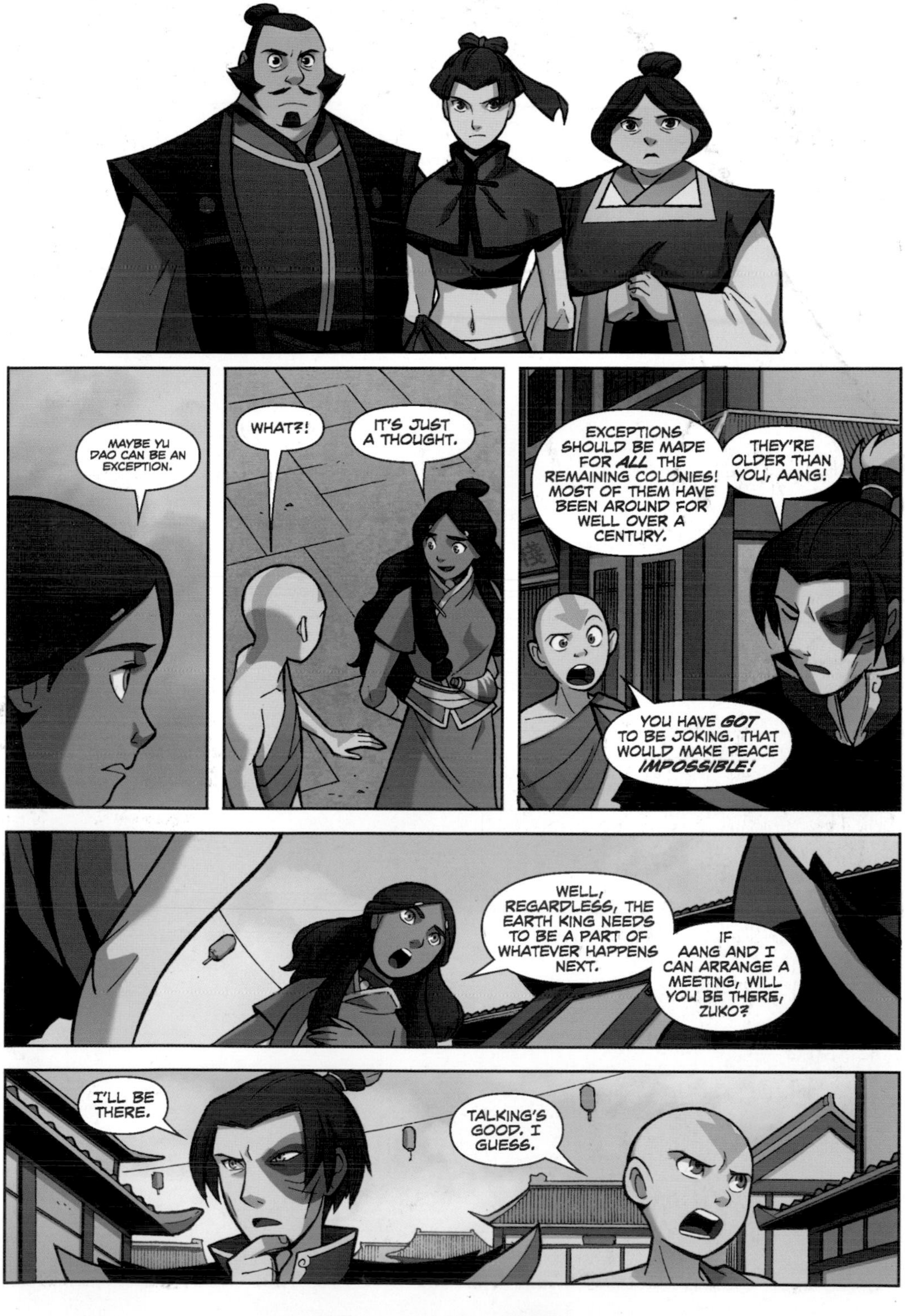
MAYBE YU DAO CAN BE AN EXCEPTION.
WHAT?!
IT'S JUST A THOUGHT.
EXCEPTIONS SHOULD BE MADE FOR *ALL* THE REMAINING COLONIES! MOST OF THEM HAVE BEEN AROUND FOR WELL OVER A CENTURY.
THEY'RE OLDER THAN YOU, AANG!
YOU HAVE *GOT* TO BE JOKING. THAT WOULD MAKE PEACE *IMPOSSIBLE!*
WELL, REGARDLESS, THE EARTH KING NEEDS TO BE A PART OF WHATEVER HAPPENS NEXT.
IF AANG AND I CAN ARRANGE A MEETING, WILL YOU BE THERE, ZUKO?
I'LL BE THERE.
TALKING'S GOOD. I GUESS.

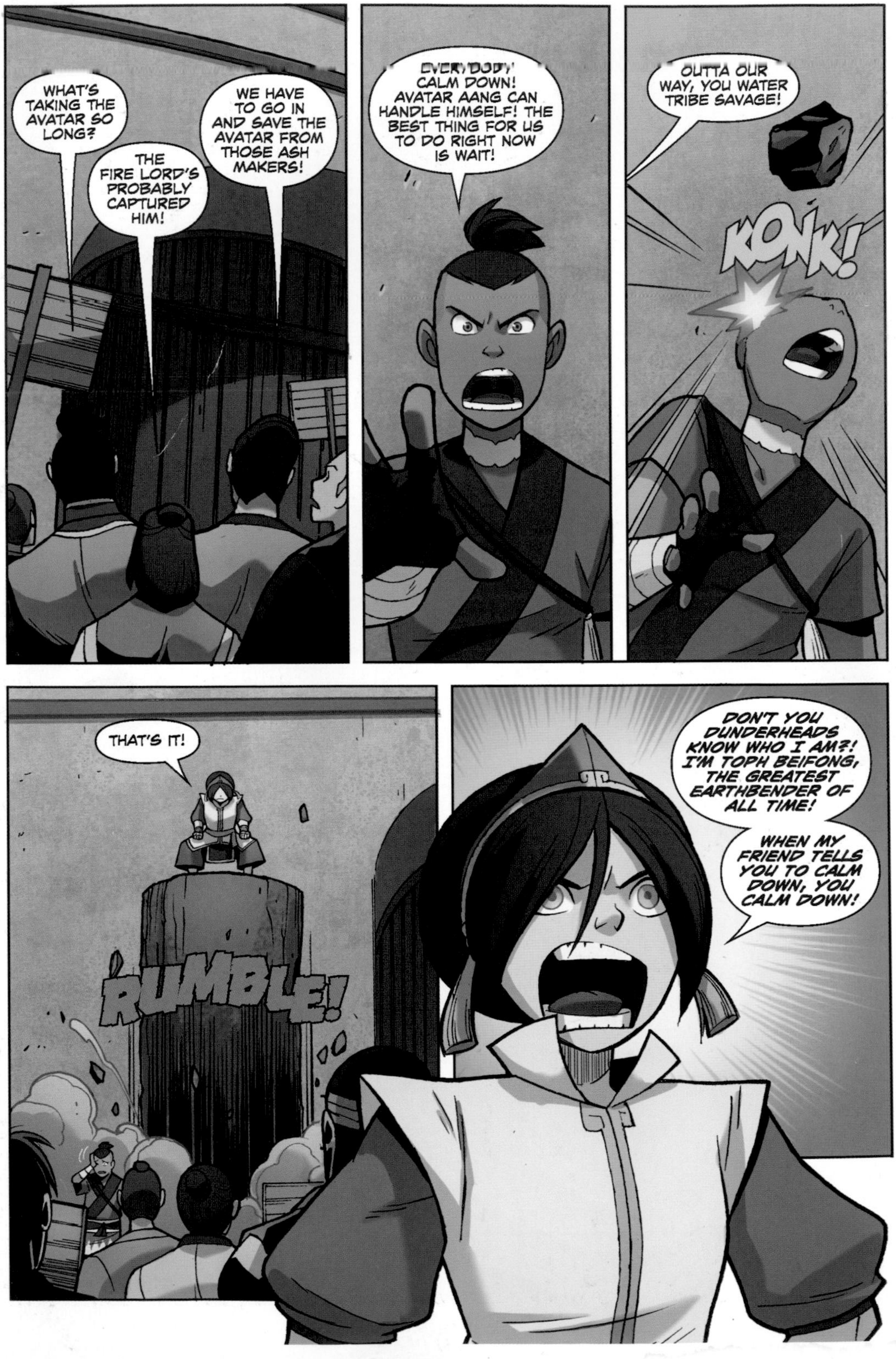
WHAT'S TAKING THE AVATAR SO LONG?
THE FIRE LORD'S PROBABLY CAPTURED HIM!
WE HAVE TO GO IN AND SAVE THE AVATAR FROM THOSE ASH MAKERS!
EVERYBODY CALM DOWN! AVATAR AANG CAN HANDLE HIMSELF! THE BEST THING FOR US TO DO RIGHT NOW IS WAIT!
OUTTA OUR WAY, YOU WATER TRIBE SAVAGE!
KONK!
THAT'S IT!
RUMBLE!
DON'T YOU DUNDERHEADS KNOW WHO I AM?! I'M TOPH BEIFONG, THE GREATEST EARTHBENDER OF ALL TIME!
WHEN MY FRIEND TELLS YOU TO CALM DOWN, YOU CALM DOWN!

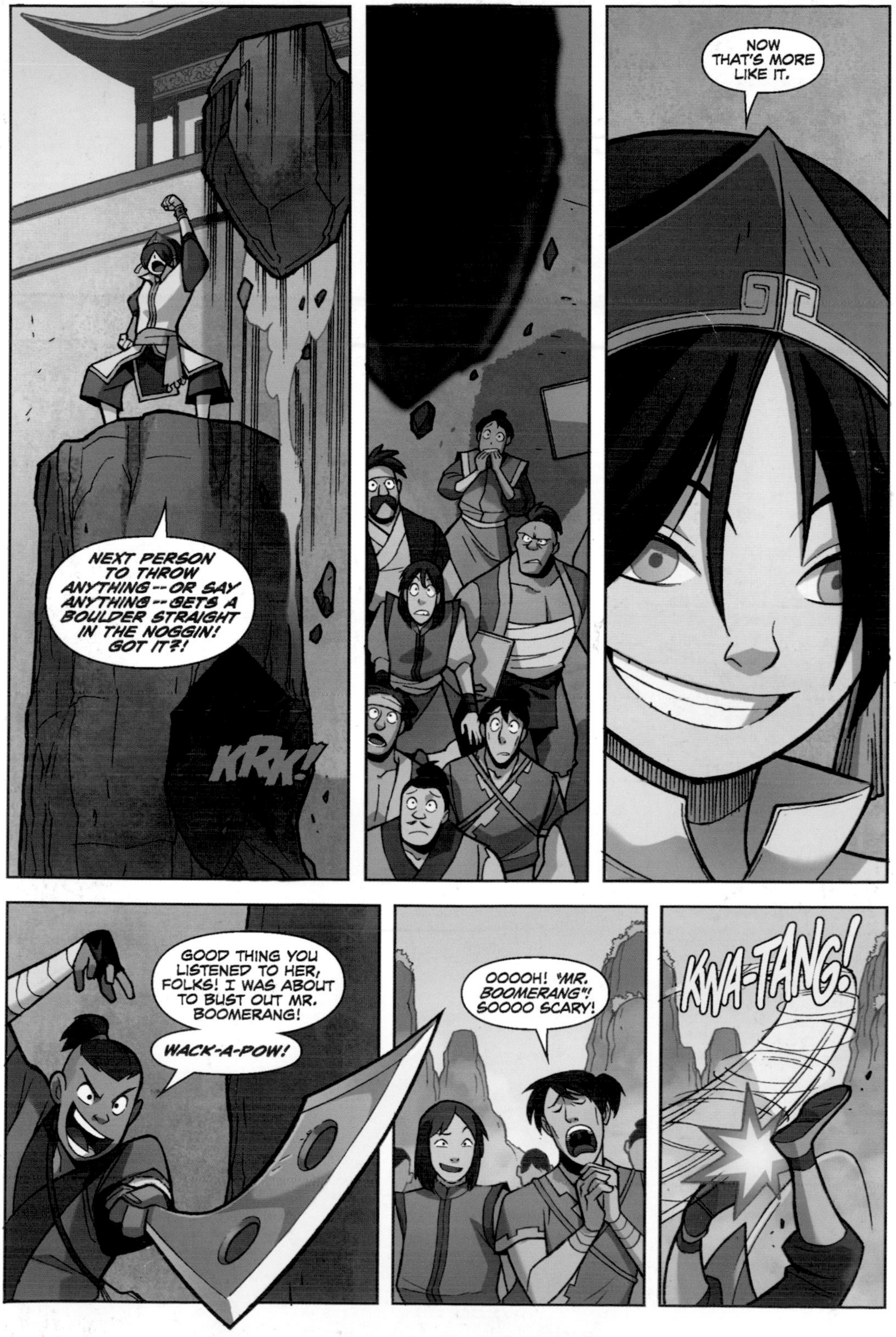
NEXT PERSON TO THROW ANYTHING--OR SAY ANYTHING--GETS A BOULDER STRAIGHT IN THE NOGGIN! GOT IT?!
KRK!
NOW THAT'S MORE LIKE IT.
GOOD THING YOU LISTENED TO HER, FOLKS! I WAS ABOUT TO BUST OUT MR. BOOMERANG!
WACK-A-POW!
OOOOH! "MR. BOOMERANG"! SOOOO SCARY!
KWA-TANG!

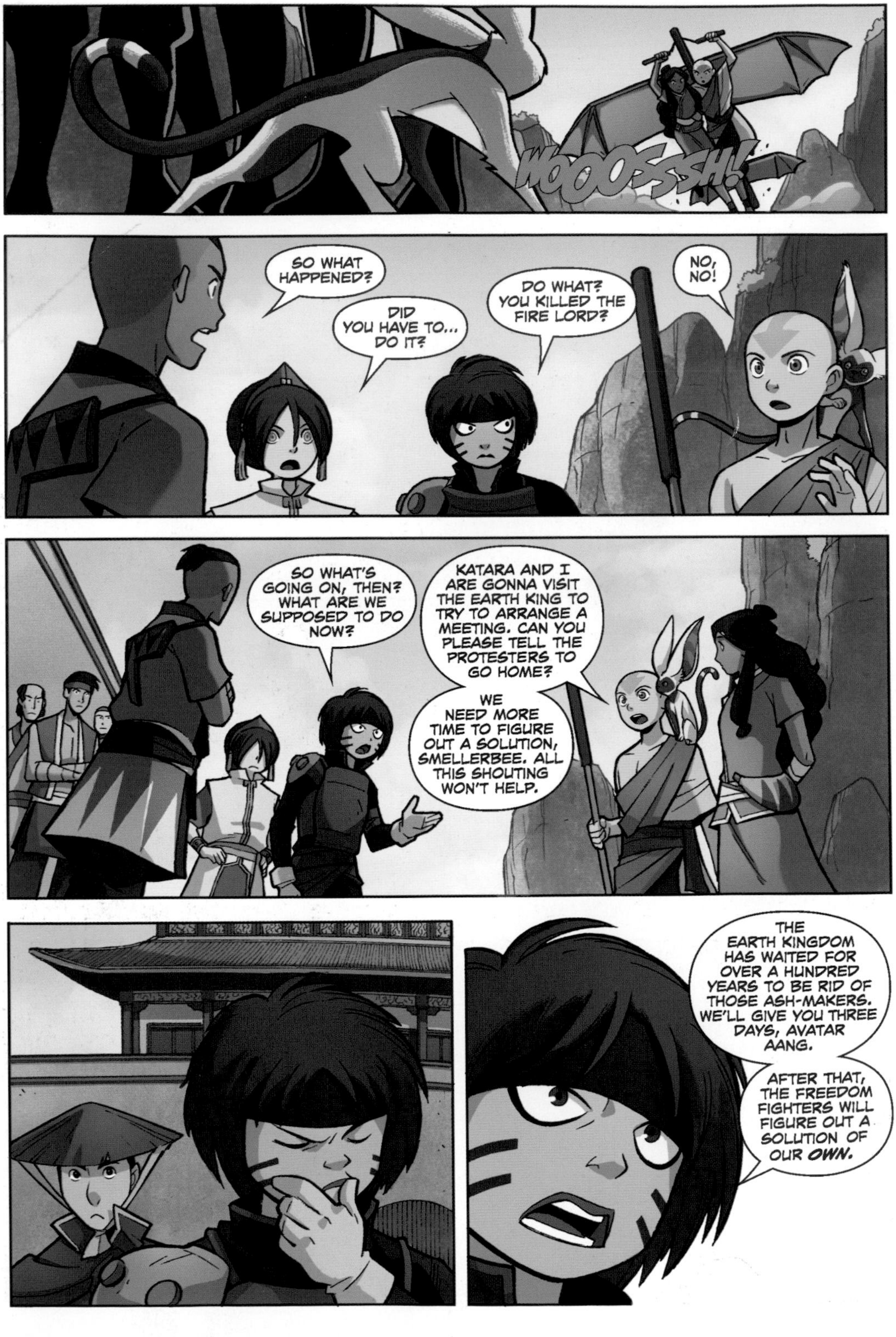
WOOOSSSH!
SO WHAT HAPPENED?
DID YOU HAVE TO... DO IT?
DO WHAT? YOU KILLED THE FIRE LORD?
NO, NO!
SO WHAT'S GOING ON, THEN? WHAT ARE WE SUPPOSED TO DO NOW?
KATARA AND I ARE GONNA VISIT THE EARTH KING TO TRY TO ARRANGE A MEETING. CAN YOU PLEASE TELL THE PROTESTERS TO GO HOME?
WE NEED MORE TIME TO FIGURE OUT A SOLUTION, SMELLERBEE. ALL THIS SHOUTING WON'T HELP.
THE EARTH KINGDOM HAS WAITED FOR OVER A HUNDRED YEARS TO BE RID OF THOSE ASH-MAKERS. WE'LL GIVE YOU THREE DAYS, AVATAR AANG.
AFTER THAT, THE FREEDOM FIGHTERS WILL FIGURE OUT A SOLUTION OF OUR *OWN*.

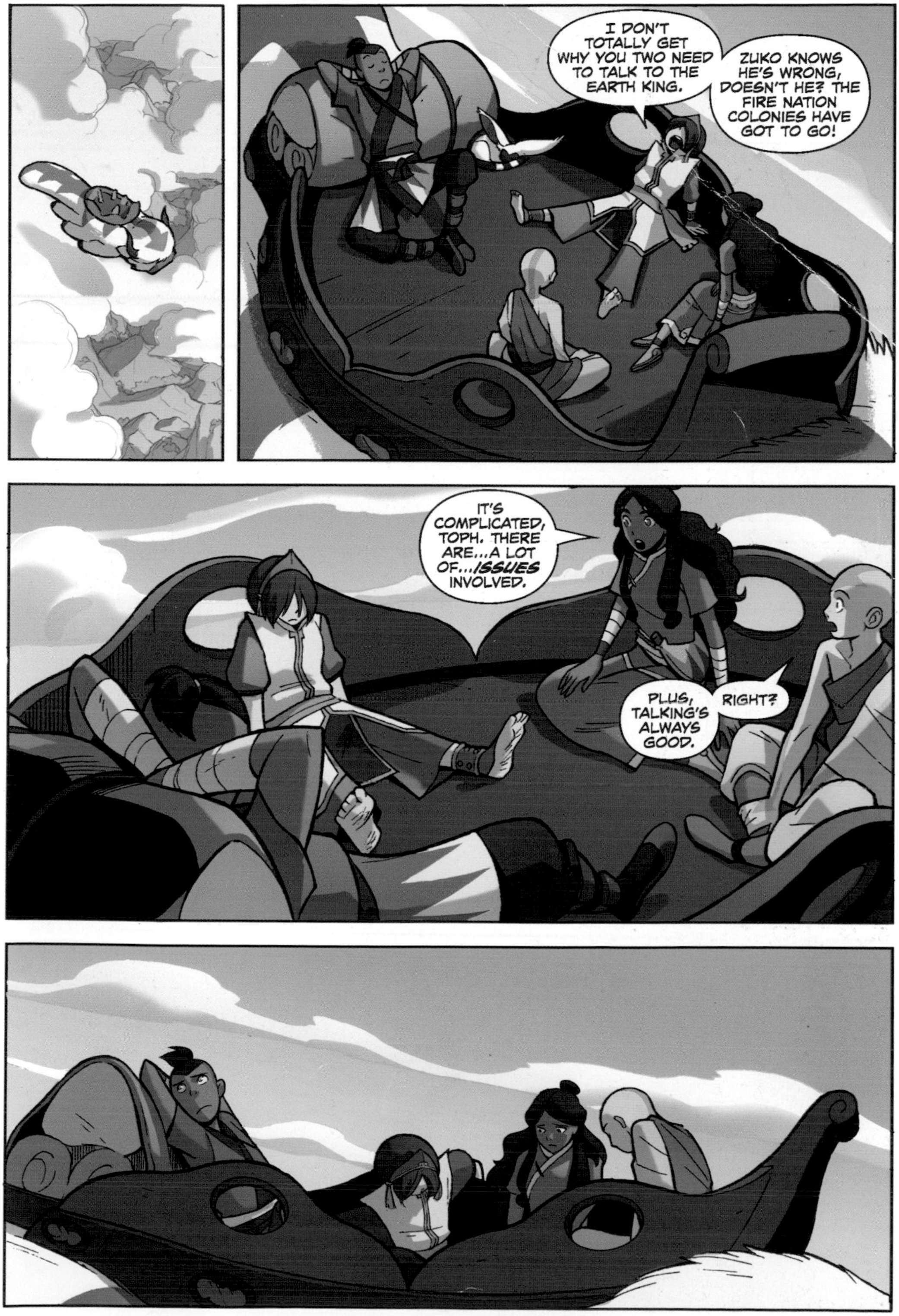
I DON'T TOTALLY GET WHY YOU TWO NEED TO TALK TO THE EARTH KING.
ZUKO KNOWS HE'S WRONG, DOESN'T HE? THE FIRE NATION COLONIES HAVE GOT TO GO!
IT'S COMPLICATED, TOPH. THERE ARE...A LOT OF...*ISSUES* INVOLVED.
PLUS, TALKING'S ALWAYS GOOD.
RIGHT?

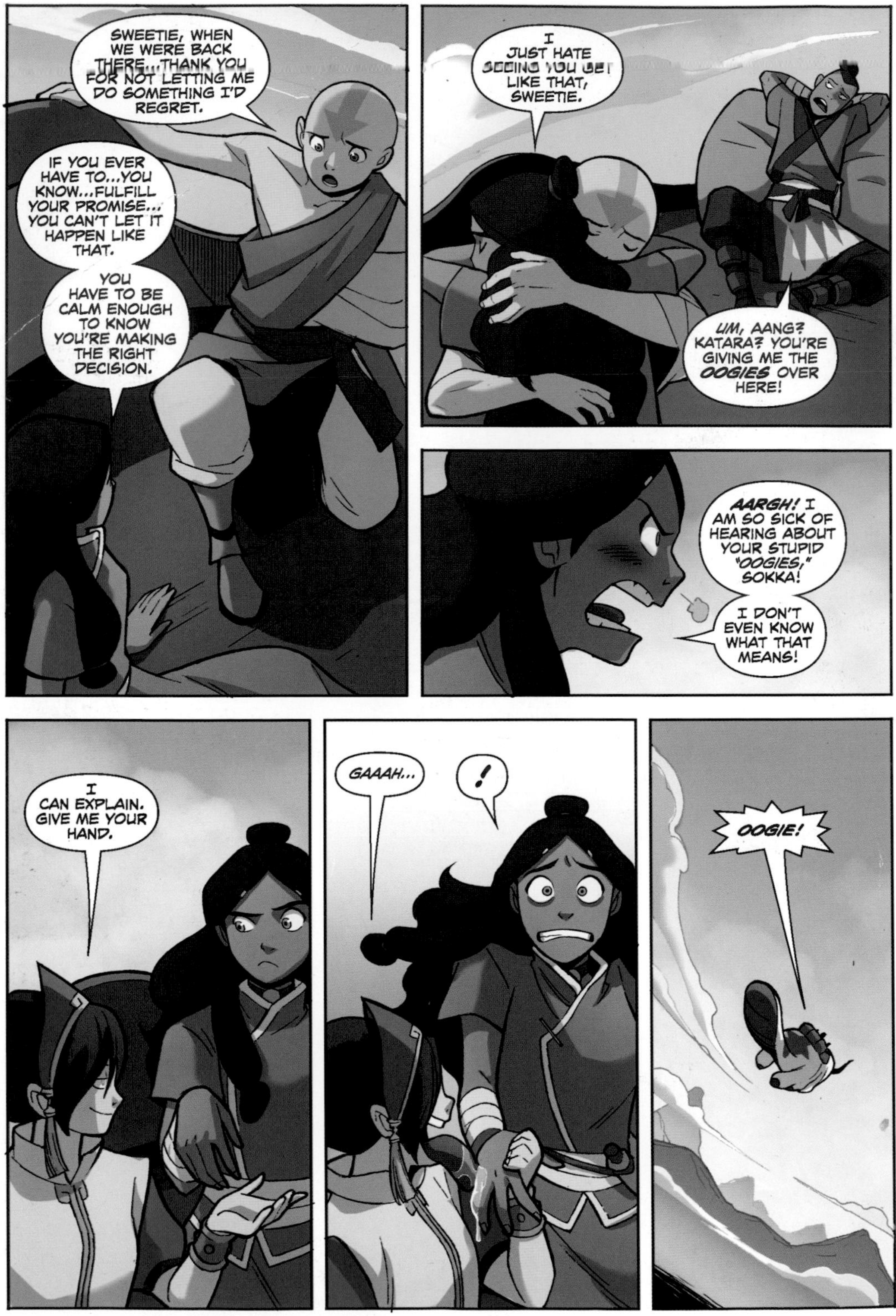
SWEETIE, WHEN WE WERE BACK THERE...THANK YOU FOR NOT LETTING ME DO SOMETHING I'D REGRET.
IF YOU EVER HAVE TO...YOU KNOW...FULFILL YOUR PROMISE... YOU CAN'T LET IT HAPPEN LIKE THAT.
YOU HAVE TO BE CALM ENOUGH TO KNOW YOU'RE MAKING THE RIGHT DECISION.
I JUST HATE SEEING YOU BE LIKE THAT, SWEETIE.
UM, AANG? KATARA? YOU'RE GIVING ME THE OOGIES OVER HERE!
AARGH! I AM SO SICK OF HEARING ABOUT YOUR STUPID "OOGIES," SOKKA!
I DON'T EVEN KNOW WHAT THAT MEANS!
I CAN EXPLAIN. GIVE ME YOUR HAND.
GAAAH...
!
OOGIE!

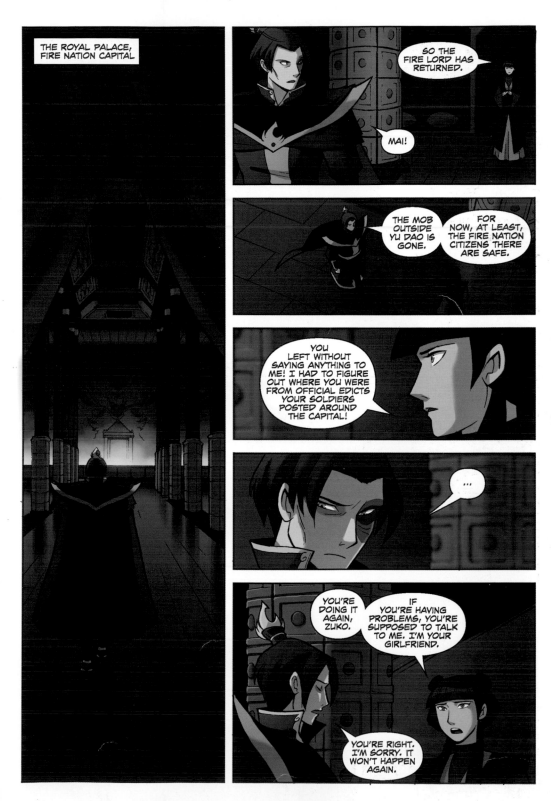

THE ROYAL PALACE, FIRE NATION CAPITAL

SO THE FIRE LORD HAS RETURNED.

MAI!

THE MOB OUTSIDE YU DAO IS GONE.

FOR NOW, AT LEAST, THE FIRE NATION CITIZENS THERE ARE SAFE.

YOU LEFT WITHOUT SAYING ANYTHING TO ME! I HAD TO FIGURE OUT WHERE YOU WERE FROM OFFICIAL EDICTS YOUR SOLDIERS POSTED AROUND THE CAPITAL!

...

YOU'RE DOING IT AGAIN, ZUKO.

IF YOU'RE HAVING PROBLEMS, YOU'RE SUPPOSED TO TALK TO ME. I'M YOUR GIRLFRIEND.

YOU'RE RIGHT. I'M SORRY. IT WON'T HAPPEN AGAIN.

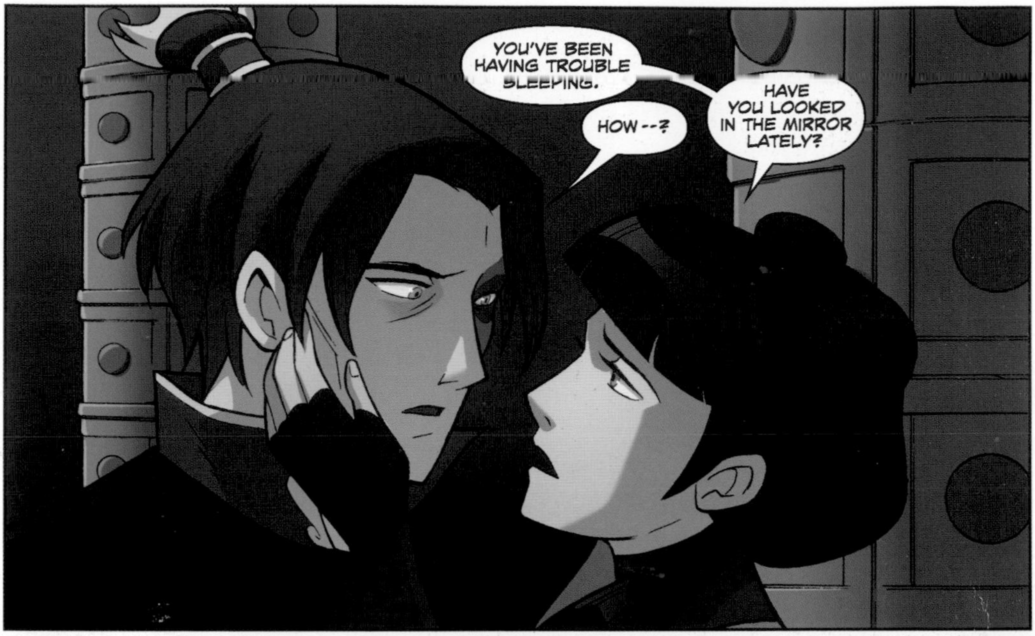
YOU'VE BEEN HAVING TROUBLE SLEEPING.
HOW--?
HAVE YOU LOOKED IN THE MIRROR LATELY?

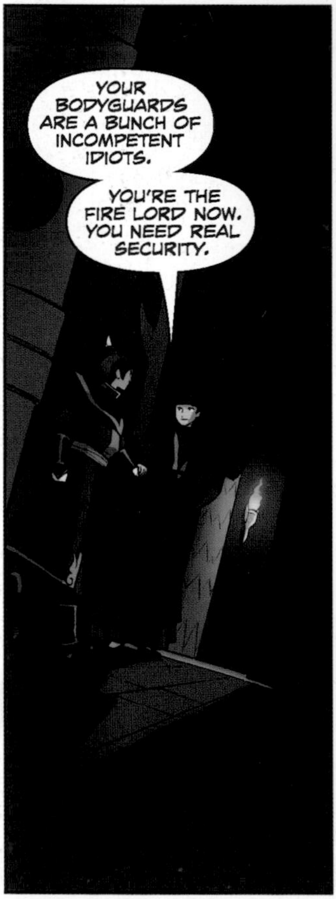
YOUR BODYGUARDS ARE A BUNCH OF INCOMPETENT IDIOTS.
YOU'RE THE FIRE LORD NOW. YOU NEED REAL SECURITY.

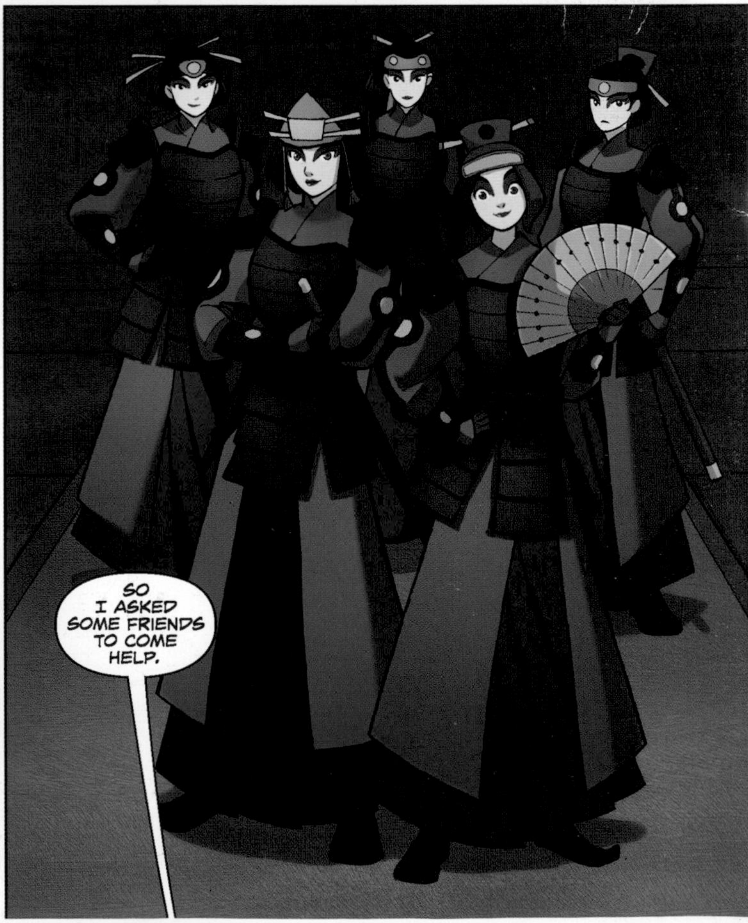
SO I ASKED SOME FRIENDS TO COME HELP.

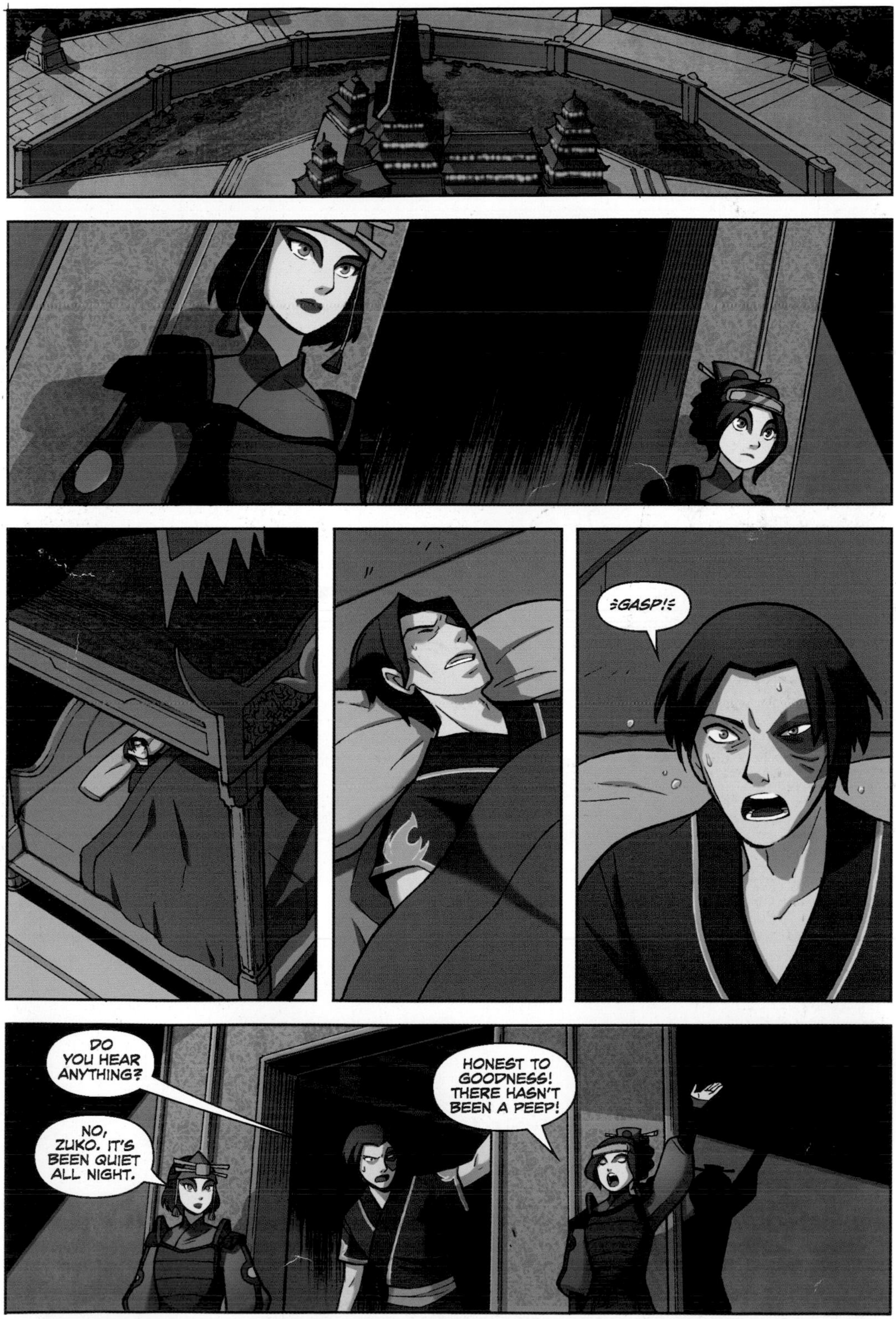

≈GASP!≈
DO YOU HEAR ANYTHING?
NO, ZUKO. IT'S BEEN QUIET ALL NIGHT.
HONEST TO GOODNESS! THERE HASN'T BEEN A PEEP!

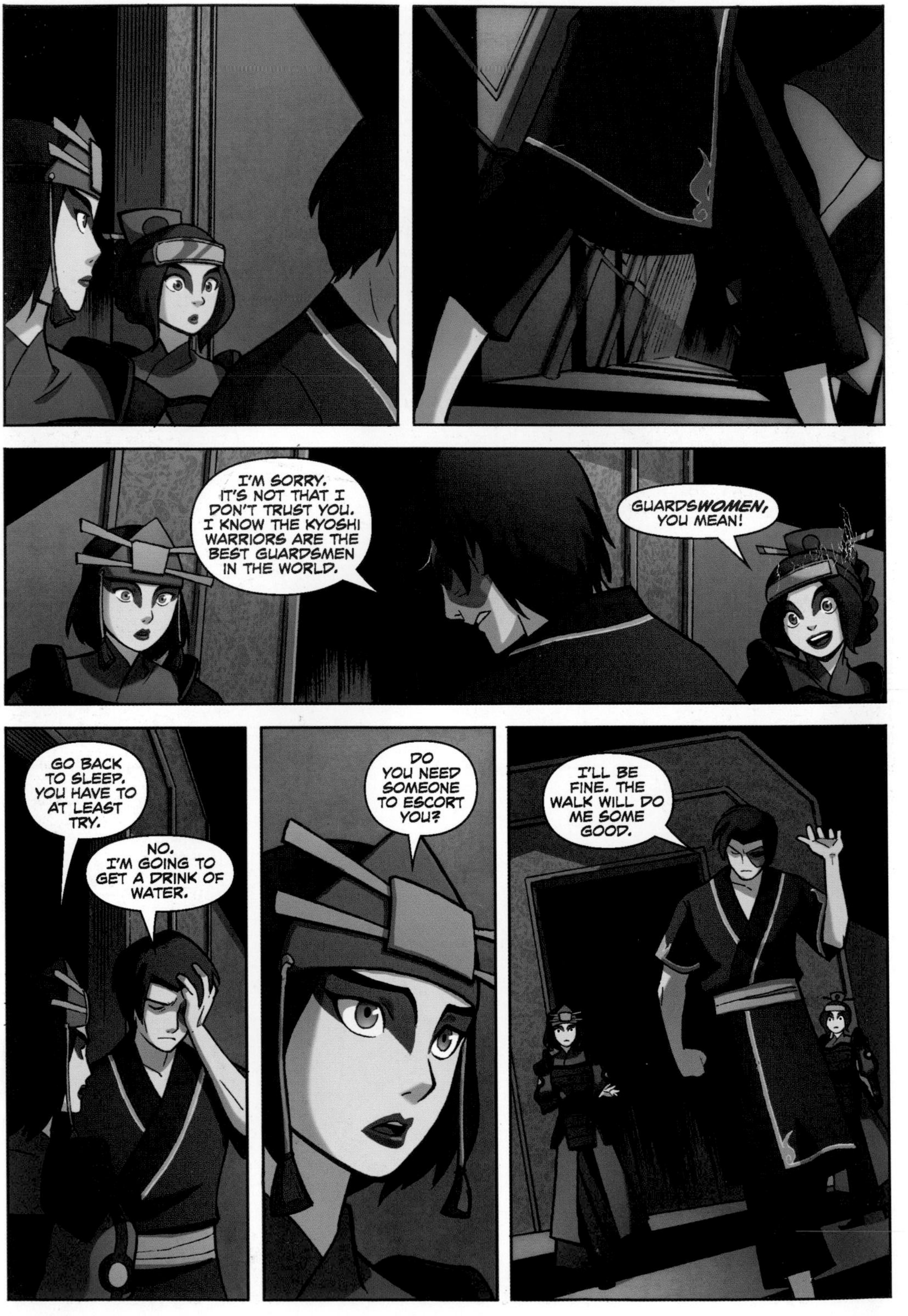
I'M SORRY. IT'S NOT THAT I DON'T TRUST YOU. I KNOW THE KYOSHI WARRIORS ARE THE BEST GUARDSMEN IN THE WORLD.
GUARDSWOMEN, YOU MEAN!
GO BACK TO SLEEP. YOU HAVE TO AT LEAST TRY.
NO. I'M GOING TO GET A DRINK OF WATER.
DO YOU NEED SOMEONE TO ESCORT YOU?
I'LL BE FINE. THE WALK WILL DO ME SOME GOOD.

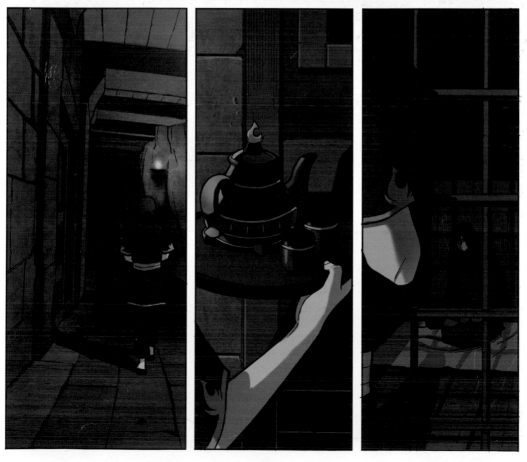

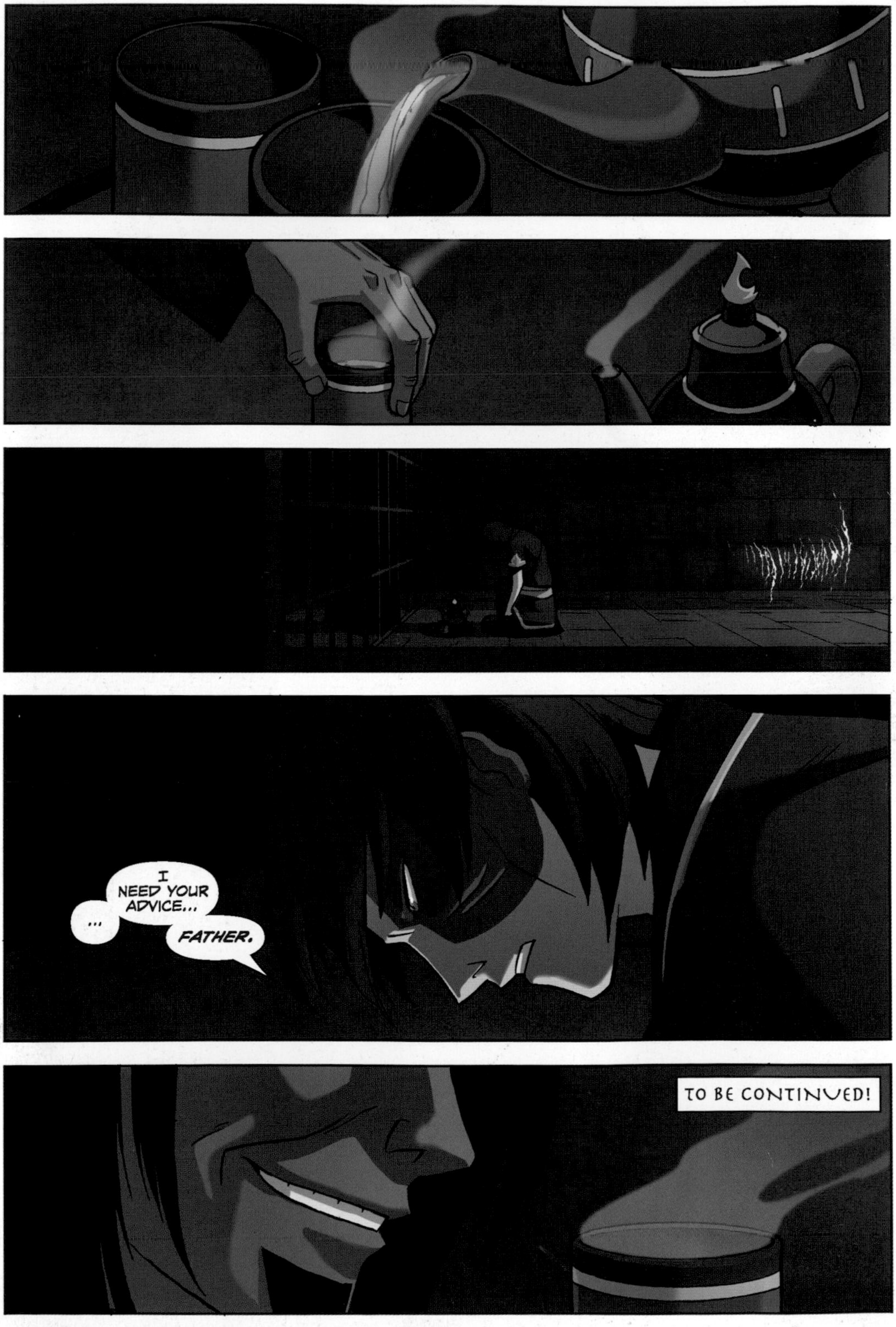
I NEED YOUR ADVICE...
...
FATHER.
TO BE CONTINUED!

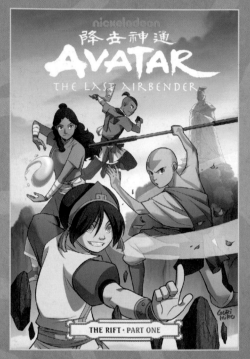
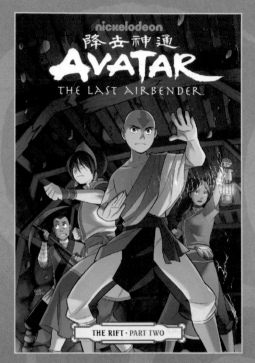

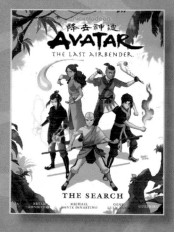

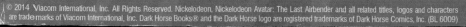